GOD ALIVE

Priorities in
Pastoral Theology

Graham Leonard
Bishop of London

Darton, Longman and Todd
London

First published 1981
by Darton, Longman & Todd Ltd
89 Lillie Road
London SW6 1UD

© Graham Leonard 1981

ISBN 0 232 51503 4

British Library Cataloguing in Publication Data

Leonard, Graham
  God alive.
  1. Pastoral theology
  I. Title
  253   BV4011

ISBN 0–232–51503–4

Printed in Great Britain by The Anchor Press Ltd
and bound by Wm. Brendon and Son Ltd
both of Tiptree, Essex

To the

Parish Priests of the

Diocese of Truro

with

respect and affection

CONTENTS

ACKNOWLEDGEMENTS

The extract from 'Choruses from "The Rock" ' by T. S. Eliot (*Collected Poems 1909–1962*) is reproduced by permission of Faber and Faber and Harcourt Brace Jovanovich Inc. The extract from *The Mind and Heart of Love* by Martin D'Arcy is reproduced by permission of Faber and Faber.

Scriptural quotations are taken from The Jerusalem Bible (copyright © 1966, 1967 and 1968 by Darton, Longman and Todd Ltd, and Doubleday and Company Inc.) and used by permission of the publishers.

The poem on p. 38 is reprinted by permission of the publishers and the Trustees of Amherst College from *The Poems of Emily Dickinson*, edited by Thomas H. Johnson, Cambridge, Mass.: Harvard University Press, Copyright © 1951, 1955, 1979 by the President and Fellows of Harvard College.

Scriptural quotations are taken from The Jerusalem Bible (copyright © 1966, 1967 and 1968 by Darton, Longman and Todd Ltd, and Doubleday and Company Inc.) and used by permission of the publishers.

PREFACE

When I was invited to give the Pastoral Theology Lectures for 1980 in the University of Durham, and reflected upon the approach I might adopt, I was of a mind to examine the pastoral theology of St Paul—particularly as seen in his pastoral care for the Christians at Corinth—and to relate it to the pastoral problems of the Church today. Such an approach, I felt, might help us to understand and to remedy the recognized gap which exists at the present time between the theologian and the pastor.

I decided to set my remarks in the context of the church at Corinth because it seemed to me that there were certain parallels between the situation there and that in Britain today. The recovery and maintenance of unity within the Body of Christ, the relationship between authority and freedom in the Spirit, marriage discipline, and antinomianism were among the problems which St Paul had to face. They are also among the problems we face today. But as I examined them and the way in which St Paul dealt with them, it proved necessary to consider also the underlying assumptions held by the Christians in Corinth in the light of which they received and reacted to the direction and guidance which St Paul gave them. It became apparent that, while some of these assumptions or underlying attitudes are still evident among Christians, in other respects there are significant differences. For this reason, while the gospel which St Paul preached and its implications for Christian life and conduct remain the same and of perennial validity, the manner in which it is communicated and the pastoral care which it demands must take account of the prevailing attitudes of contemporary men and women and of the society in which they live. If such attitudes are not examined critically, and the appropriate Christian response discerned, very soon the demands of the gospel are regarded as impossible or irrelevant and calls are heard with increasing insistence and shrillness for their modification to meet the needs of contemporary thought.

I begin, therefore, with the church in Corinth and then consider the prevailing attitudes of today in the hope that this will enable us to determine what our priorities in pastoral theology must be if we are both to be faithful to the gospel and to take account of the world in which we live and in which we are called to proclaim it.

I am very grateful to the Senate of the University of Durham for the invitation to deliver the Lectures. I shall always remember the generous welcome and hospitality which was given to me by the members of the Faculty of Theology and which made my stay in Durham so enjoyable and stimulating.

July 1981   + Graham Londin:

CHAPTER 1

On reading the letters of St Paul it is difficult to avoid the impression that he regards what we would describe as pastoral theology as a regrettable necessity. He repeatedly affirms that his prime vocation is to preach the gospel. He describes himself as 'Paul, a servant of Christ Jesus, who has been called to be an apostle and specially chosen to preach the Good News that God promised long ago through his prophets in the Scriptures'.[1] Yet from the outset it proves impossible for him to fulfil his vocation by being no more than an itinerant evangelist. Although St Paul himself is so seized by the glory, love and mercy of God that the implications of the gospel seem obvious and compelling, his converts do not see it in quite the same light. For one reason or another, they need to be reminded, cajoled, inspired, guided, rebuked and taught. St Paul does not resent the demands which they make upon him, though he does not minimize them and at times it is clear that he finds it hard to be patient. His burning love for God and his converts and his passionate zeal make him willing to be spent in their service and he does not shrink from putting his own reputation at risk if their needs demand it.

The first chapter of his letter to the Galatians, probably the earliest to survive, refers to the pastoral problems which he had to face following his preaching of the gospel. One purpose of that letter was to deal with 'the trouble-makers among them who wanted to change the Good News of

Christ',[2] but the autobiographical passage in Chapter 2 reveals that he had already had to face the pastoral problems of the circumcision of Titus and the abandonment by St Peter of his practice of eating with the Gentiles. For St Paul, both issues were far more than the personal dilemmas of individuals. In both, the action which was at stake would, in St Paul's judgement, have compromised an essential element in the gospel. The requirement that Titus should be circumcised imperilled the liberty which Christ brought because it imposed the requirement of the Law in this respect on a Gentile. For St Peter, to eat only with Jewish Christians and not with Gentiles was to fail to respect the true meaning of the Good News which proclaims that all are one in Christ Jesus.

The letters of St Paul were all written to meet pastoral situations and manifest his passionate concern that the life of the Church and the lives of individual Christians should reflect the gospel. Even the letter to the Christians in Rome, which is the nearest to a theological treatise rather than a letter, is deeply pastoral in its approach. 'The reason why I have written to you and put some things rather strongly', he says, 'is to refresh your memories, since God has given me this special position. He has appointed me a priest of Jesus Christ, and I am to carry out my priestly duty by bringing the Good News from God to the pagans, and so make them acceptable as an offering made holy by the Holy Spirit.'[3] His letter reflects the need which he experienced to draw out the implications of the gospel both for the Christian community and for the individual. He is concerned to make it clear that the way a Christian lives and behaves is derived from the doctrinal content of the gospel and that if the latter is misunderstood or distorted the effect will be evident in behaviour. The doctrinal content includes the meaning of those acts of grace, Baptism and Holy Communion, by which they were incorporated into Christ and are sustained in their union with him.

St Paul achieves his purpose both by the way in which he

expounds the doctrinal content and by specific spiritual and moral direction. When he gives such direction, it is usually prefaced by 'wherefore', 'for this reason' or some such phrase to make evident its connection with his doctrinal teaching. In Romans 12:1, St Paul uses not only 'therefore' but also 'by the mercies of God' to introduce his appeal to his readers to offer themselves as a living sacrifice. The phrase 'by the mercies of God' can be understood both as referring to the nature of God as revealed in his acts in Christ and to the fact that it is through those acts that the offering is made possible. The nature of God as merciful both draws us in loving obedience and enables us. Both 'therefore' and 'by the mercies of God' refer back to the exposition of the gospel in the previous chapters and look forward to the doxology with which the letter ends:

> Glory to him who is able to give you the strength to live according to the Good News I preach, and in which I proclaim Jesus Christ, the revelation of a mystery kept secret for endless ages, but now so clear that it must be broadcast to pagans everywhere to bring them to the obedience of faith. This is only what scripture has predicted, and it is all part of the way God wants things to be. He alone is Wisdom; give glory therefore to him through Jesus Christ for ever and ever. Amen.[4]

St Paul also frequently appeals to his readers to remember what they are by grace. In Romans 6 he reminds them of what they have been taught about the meaning of their baptism and develops it in terms of death to sin and new life in Christ. So, in the first letter to the Corinthians, he draws out in precise and concrete terms the implications of their membership of the Body of Christ by baptism. 'You know, surely, that your bodies are members making up the body of Christ; do you think I can take parts of Christ's body and join them to the body of a prostitute. Never!'[5] Again he sees the fact that in the Eucharist the bread we break is a communion with the Body of Christ as forbidding any compromise with idolatry. The purpose of receiving the fruit of a sacrifice was communion with the god to whom it was offered. As they received the fruit of the sacrifice of Christ they were in communion with him and so should not be in communion with demons.[6]

The need for the Good News to be proclaimed is dominant in the thought of St Paul. Although his letters are full of compassion, sympathy and concern, the needs of the converts are secondary to the need for the love, mercy and holiness of God to be made evident. He continually emphasizes that that which is consonant with the Good News and with the nature of God revealed in the Good News brings salvation, joy and freedom, even when it demands suffering. In other words, there is for St Paul no contradiction between showing true compassion and proclaiming the demands of God, and he does not shrink from facing the difference between living according to our fallen nature and walking in the Spirit.

Turning to the Christian community in Corinth, there are several situations which St Paul has to face which have points of similarity with those we face today. Unity within the Body of Christ, authority, the spiritualizing of the gospel, freedom in the Spirit, antinomianism and marriage discipline are all issues to be found in the church in Corinth and issues today of which few pastors have not had experience. Of these, three, namely unity, spiritualizing the gospel, and freedom in the Spirit, will be considered.

First there is the problem of the unity of the Church. It is not suggested that the divisions in Corinth can be directly compared with our denominational divisions in Britain today. The latter owe their origin to historical, cultural and social causes which did not apply in Corinth, as well as to differences in theology (though it must not be supposed that non-theological causes have not had a profound effect on the unity of the Church at all times including the first few centuries).[7] The situation in Corinth does, however, remind us of two fundamental aspects of the problem of unity. The first is that unity within the local congregation is as much a matter of concern as unity between churches or congregations. It is not surprising if a church which is at disunity within itself finds it difficult to live in unity or achieve unity with other churches. Moreover, it is within a disunited Church that the non-theological factors are most likely to have effect. Secondly, in the letter to the Corinthians the moral aspect of unity is emphasized. However much disunity may be due to doctrinal or cultural differences, there is always present the disruptive element of self-will which must be dealt with as a root cause.

A radical approach to Christian unity must begin by considering the element of self-will which exists at both the individual and the corporate level. As St Paul makes clear, the unity of the Church is given by God and it is self-will which prevents that unity from being expressed and implemented in the life of the community.

The disunity at Corinth expresses itself in various ways. It shows itself in allegiance given to parties of people rather than to the Lord as Head of the Church. It shows itself in spiritual arrogance and the despising of those who do not possess a particular gift. It shows itself in moral indifference to the life of the community. In the case of incest, with which St Paul deals in Chapter 5 of the first letter, he directs his most severe words to the community for tolerating the presence of such immorality within the Church without call for repentance. It shows itself in an insensitivity towards the scandal which may be caused by actions which are lawful but not expedient. It shows itself in a disregard of the fact that the individual Christian is part of the Body of Christ and that what he does with his body affects the whole Christian community. It shows itself in an assertion of individual rights by appeal to the secular courts. It shows itself in individualistic and disruptive behaviour at the Eucharist. It shows itself in envy and in an unwillingness to accept the diversity of the gifts of the Spirit.

Each of those expressions of disunity is reflected in some

way or other in the life of the Church today. In dealing with them St Paul's main thrust lies in his reaffirmation of the need for death and resurrection as the way to the re-creation of all things in Christ. His most substantial consideration of this relates to the death and resurrection of Christ himself in Chapter 15 of 1 Corinthians, but he also emphasizes it in relation to the nature of the body into which they have been baptized, of which love must be the supreme quality. In Chapter 15 he says 'I want to remind you of the gospel I preached to you' and then stresses both the centrality of the cross and resurrection of Christ and the death and resurrection which every man must experience in Christ. What he says in that chapter reflects what he has said in Chapter 1 about the crucified Christ's being the power and wisdom of God. It also looks forward to the magnificent description of his apostolate in terms of dying to live in the third and fourth chapters of 2 Corinthians. Disunity is presented by St Paul as having its origins in an evasion of the cross. This characteristic of the church in Corinth is one which it shares with the Church today. It will be discussed more fully later as St Paul sees the same cause leading to the second issue which he faced there, namely the spiritualization of the gospel.

The origins of Gnosticism, the extent to which it had developed at the time of the apostolic Church and its relationships with Christianity are matters of acute debate. Nevertheless, whether or not Gnosticism is regarded as a heretical development existing in Judaism which was picked up and used within the Church, it is clear that St Paul had to deal at Corinth and elsewhere with those within the Church who held views similar to those professed by Gnostics. These saw salvation as lying in the acquisition of spiritual knowledge. Gnosticism rejected the possibility of any direct relationship between the divine and the created. The hidden wisdom known to the Gnostic enabled him at death to escape from the created order and be exalted to the divine realm. To quote Professor John Ruef:

In the Christian version of Gnosticism, this knowledge is brought to man by the redeemer, Jesus, who descends from heaven, takes human form, transmits the saving knowledge of man, and then leaving his human form to its ignominious fate, ascends, as all good Gnostics do, to the realm of pure divinity.[8]

Gnosticism not only denies the reality of the incarnation but replaces the saving death and resurrection of Christ by an exaltation into the divine realm. By contrast, St Paul first emphasizes that true knowledge and wisdom are to be found in the cross, not in human speculation, and refers ironically to the knowledge which the Christians in Corinth suppose they possess. In Chapter 15 he develops this and speaks of the true basis of Christian hope. It lies in the facts that Christ truly died as all men die and was raised from the dead. In his death the power of death was defeated and through his resurrection man is enabled to share in his glorified humanity. In Chapter 4 of the second letter St Paul develops this in terms of the life of the Christians. 'We carry with us in our body the death of Jesus, so that the life of Jesus, too, may always be seen in our body.' [9] At first sight it may seem that the speculations of Gnosticism are far removed from the life of the Church today but, as Hubert Richards reminds us, it should not be 'too easily assumed that the Gnostic perversion of Christianity with which this correspondence is so concerned, is by now a dead letter.' And he goes on:

Indeed, good gnostic sermons are preached each Sunday from many pulpits, where God and Christ are presented as living in a world unbridgeably remote from the world of men, where the divinity of Christ is so spoken of that it effectively denies his brotherhood with the rest of men, where his fleeting 'visit' among men was for the purpose of revealing to an elite a set of truths otherwise unknown to the world, and where right relationship with God consists of escaping from the body as he did, in order to preserve those heavenly truths.[10]

7

One assumption commonly made in the Church today has also something in common with the approach of Gnosticism. It is the assumption that Christian truth is *primarily* understood by the mind and that the ability of a truth to be apprehended by the human mind must be a measure of its acceptability. Mystery and paradox are regarded with suspicion, and the biblical teaching that truth is understood by doing it as well as by thinking about it is discounted.

However, a more significant link between Gnosticism and the present situation will be found by the pastoral theologian as he seeks to apply his theology. The underlying belief of Gnosticism was that no direct relationship was possible between the divine and the created, the infinite and the finite. In the case of Gnosticism this led to the isolation of esoteric knowledge as the only way to escape from the one to the other. But for different reasons the same belief underlies modern atheism. Though Descartes himself remained a convinced Christian, his *Cogito ergo sum* as developed by Kant and Hegel opened the way for the belief that 'the affirmation of God as infinite being necessarily implies the devaluation of finite being and, in particular the dehumanization of man.' [11] Particularly as a result of the thought of Ludwig Feuerbach, who maintained that the real object and adequate basis of any meaning and value disclosed to the human consciousness is human nature itself, the affirmation of God was regarded as a source of alienation and a denial of the authenticity of man. In Feuerbach's thought 'since the religious projection is essentially a transference of human properties to an illusory God, the richer the notion of God elaborated, the more man is impoverished and reduced to a miserable and servile condition.' [12] Modern atheism and Gnosticism have another point in common which will be developed later, namely, the rejection of suffering as an authentic element in human life. For these reasons, the way in which St Paul deals with the Christians in Corinth of Gnostic disposition may have more to say to the modern pastoral theologian than he supposes as he seeks to relate the gospel to

8

believers in whom is to be found what Bernard Haring calls 'hidden atheism' and who regard suffering as to be avoided at whatever cost.

A third parallel seems to lie in the matter of freedom by the Spirit. It would appear that there were in the Corinthian church at least two groups who claimed the inspiration of the Spirit for what St Paul regarded as unchristian behaviour. Those who had come under Gnostic influence—the enlightened ones—interpreted the gift of the Spirit in the modern sense of spiritual, that is non-material and as freeing them from the shackles of the flesh. On the other hand there were those who, possibly, interpreted it in an ecstatic sense; such an interpretation would be understandable in reaction against the arid intellectualism of the 'enlightened ones'. The external manifestation of Spirit-possession was speaking in tongues. Those who had received this manifestation clearly put a high value upon it and, it would seem, tended to despise those who had not, thereby contributing to the disunity of the congregation. Both groups, for different reasons, regarded the freedom of the Spirit as releasing them from any need to discipline the body. St Paul reminds them of the fact that their union with Christ extends to the body and that they are 'not free from God's law being under the law of Christ'.[13] The pastoral theologian and the pastor today face in some quarters a not dissimilar situation. There is an understandable dissatisfaction with a predominantly cerebral expression of Christian discipleship and a desire that the gospel should be experienced both corporately and individually. But all too often attempts to remedy this situation end in disaster. Anyone who has had to exercise pastoral care for first-generation Christians coming from a background which is largely amoral, knows from experience that charismatic experience can easily result in the kind of antinomianism evident in Corinth. The indiscriminate use of the Kiss of Peace in the Eucharist has, for example, led to the development of un-Christian relationships, when it has not been set in the context of clear teaching about the moral element in

9

holiness. (It is also open to the charge of being unreal when it is clearly seen not to reflect Christian charity in the relationship between the members of the Christian community outside the time of the service.) An unbalanced and undisciplined emphasis on experience can also easily merit the charge of seeking 'cheap grace', to use Bonhoeffer's famous phrase; that is, wanting the solace of religious experience without accepting the cost of true discipline. In dealing with the problems in Corinth St Paul concentrates on the reality of the union with Christ in his Body, which is the Church, and the consequent obligation of obedience to his will. He emphasizes the need for implementing the significance of the cross in the Christian life by death to self-will as the necessary way to living in union with the risen Christ. Nevertheless St Paul was not afraid to speak in terms of experience. For him the knowledge and love of God in Christ through the Spirit was a consuming experience involving his whole self. Though he emphasizes the need for understanding, knowledge is never confined to the mind. Though he stresses the need for obedience love is far more than a naked act of the will. Contemporary Christians are right to seek to experience life in Christ and are justifiably critical of attempts to play down the emotions. What matters is that emotional experience takes its rightful place within an all-embracing experience of God in which mind and will have also their rightful part. It is also important, as Martin Thornton has pointed out, to distinguish between relying on experience and expecting it.[14] To rely on experience is to forget that we are to love God because he first loved us. To expect experience is simply to take God at his word. It must, however, never be forgotten that experience of God is not to be identified with a state of euphoria in which the reality of sin and evil is ignored or denied. Our experience of God may be, and frequently is, in terms of suffering, darkness and desolation.[15]

Although these are similarities from which we can certainly learn, it is first necessary to try and compare the underlying assumptions, in the light of which the Christians

10

in Corinth received and interpreted the direction and guidance which St Paul gave them, with those held by the average Christian in this country today. If pastoral theology is to fulfil its function, it is vital that account is taken of the way in which it will be received and of the pastoral situation in which it is to be exercised. Something of a parallel can be seen in the matter of legislation. Any form of legislation must take into account the mind and will of the community to which it relates. If it does not, it will become a dead letter or be so misunderstood as to stultify the intention of the legislators. A good example is to be seen in the working of the Divorce Reform Act, which was said by its sponsors to be intended to buttress the stability of marriage and encourage reconciliation. It has certainly not fulfilled that intention, as its sponsors now recognize. This is largely due to the fact that the popular understanding of the intention of the Act was that it was passed to make divorce easier. The legislators failed to take account of the realities of human nature. The way in which it has been operated has also contributed to the way in which it has been understood. The introduction of the shortened procedure, which is, in effect, divorce by post, has encouraged the idea that divorce is available on demand. At the same time there has been a failure to recognize the effect of easier divorce on children. It must be recognized that, in the realm of pastoral theology, what may appear and be intended to be guidance based on sensitive recognition of human need is, in fact, seen as condonation or approval of actions or attitudes.

Some of the underlying assumptions or attitudes to be found in Corinth would seem to be the same as those evident today. The most obvious is probably the assumption that salvation or the achievement of one's spiritual destiny can be attained without following the way of the cross. The Corinthian Christians seemed to think that it could be attained by knowledge or by spiritual experience. This attitude can be described in another way which reflects Chapter 13 of the first letter by saying that it represents a failure to recognize

11

the ultimate nature of love and the cost of loving. An essential element in St Paul's ministry to them consisted in bringing them to suffer in God's way and thereby to repentance. Side by side with this attitude lay the assumption that holiness did not embrace moral goodness, an assumption which St Paul repeatedly refutes. Both are evident among Christians today. The former is reflected in the contemporary search for happiness based on the satisfaction of immediate desires rather than the attainment of excellence through discipline and sacrifice. At times it seems as if only those who seek excellence in the realms of the arts or athletics are prepared to accept that it involves long and demanding discipline. In the realm of personal relationships, and of marriage in particular, immediate results are expected. This attitude will be discussed more fully in the next chapter. The second assumption is reflected not so much in the fact that Christians are more sinful than they used to be, as that, acting in a way which is clearly contrary to the teaching and example of our Lord, they claim divine sanction for doing so. It is the sad experience of some bishops that not only lay people but also priests are unwilling to resist the pressures of infatuation and desert their wives and families, brazenly claiming that because they are 'in love' it is the will of God that they should do so. If attention is drawn to our Lord's teaching, the reply received is that it does not apply in the particular person's case or, as in one instance in my own experience, in the bland statement that in this matter our Lord was wrong.

There are, however, two respects in which I think there is a fundamental difference between the assumptions of the Corinthian Christians and Christians today.

The first concerns the way in which people think about the relationship between 'being' and 'doing'. It could be described as the difference between the 'ontological' and the 'functional' approaches to existence, but for two reasons the simpler words are to be preferred. First, 'ontology' has a clearly defined philosophical meaning and to use it in a wider and more general sense can be confusing. Secondly, the use of the word 'ontological' is frequently misunderstood and taken to imply that, in addition to affirming the priority of 'being' as compared with 'doing', a particular way of talking metaphysically about 'being' is taken for granted. It is possible to affirm that 'being' comes before 'doing' without implying the acceptance of any particular way of describing 'being'.

The ancient, be he Greek or Hebrew, was aware that he existed and that his activity proceeded from his existence. Activity was seen as the process of becoming what he already was. He found himself to be a part of the created universe. He had not created himself nor had he created the world. What mattered was that he knew what he was as a human being so that he could live in a way which expressed and implemented that nature. He also had to learn the forces and laws of Nature if he were to live within it and as part of it. As Professor R. H. Fuller has written, 'It is not just a quirk of the Greek mind but a universal human apperception that action implies prior being—even if, as is also true, being is only apprehended in action.'[16] In recent years thinking in this way has become philosophically unfashionable. It is also a way which is alien to the mind of modern man.

The reasons for this change of attitude are complex and obscure in their relationships to each other. In one sense, as Feuerbach perceived, it is but a logical development of the Cartesian standpoint. *Cogito ergo sum*: 'I think, therefore I am' leads very easily into the belief that my existence depends upon my thought rather than that my ability to reflect is evidence of my existence as a person. It is sometimes supposed that the change of attitude is due largely to the development of the theory of evolution, but the process had already begun before Darwin's theory was published in 1859. Certainly the idea was strengthened by that theory, encouraging as it did the idea that the created universe, instead of being 'given' and 'fixed', was in the process of becoming. Natural selection, however, which was the basis of Darwin's theory and remains the basis of the modern theory of evolution, is not incompatible with a view of 'being' as prior to 'action'. Natural selection is the process by which those organisms which by their nature are most fitted to adapt to changing circumstances survive and propagate their kind. Evolution by natural selection can properly be described as the survival of the fittest depending upon qualities which are inborn. Neo-Darwinism is based both upon the Mendelian process of assorting genes which provides the variants upon which natural selection works and upon random mutations which alone provide new genes. Which variations are beneficial for evolutionary development depends on the environment. This does not alter the fact that the process operates on the basis of what an organism is, from which its behaviour derives. Environment works on the material which is available and does not create it. The unpopularity of the belief that 'being' is prior to 'action' receives support from the way in which evolution is frequently presented, as for example, in popular programmes on the media. Prior to Darwin, evolution was thought to proceed by the inheritance of acquired characteristics. Thus it was held that a giraffe acquired the genetic code for a long neck through generations of feeding upon the leaves of the upper branches of trees. This theory, known as Lamarckism, has not been supported by observation and experiment and has been discredited by modern molecular biology which knows of no method by which changes in an organism in its lifetime can affect its genetic mechanism. Yet evolution is constantly presented at the popular level in Lamarckian terms, thereby giving the impression that 'being' is determined by 'doing'. Another reason for the rejection of the priority of 'being' lies in industrialization and technological development with its divorce between man and nature. This is partly due to the fact that the effects of a particular process may be, and are likely to be, far removed in space and time from those who are responsible for it. As a result, man ceases to be aware of the effects of his actions, and particularly of the effect which they have upon the balance of nature. Even a farmer may

14

not become aware for some years of the side-effects of the use of some product of technological development. It is not surprising that a man working in a factory producing insecticides should be unaware of the effect they may have upon the environment. As a result we acquire the frame of mind which sees nature as there simply to be used for man's ends without taking account of what it is and of its qualities which must be respected.

Two other factors complicate the situation. The development of *social* evolution is Lamarckian in character. At the human level, it is possible for acquired wisdom to be handed on from generation to generation and for cultures to be formed. Such wisdom is not acquired by the individual at birth. The new-born human young has less inborn instincts than the young of other creatures and has to acquire them through family and social life. It is, however, very easy to confuse the two modes of development. This can happen either by concentrating on a rigid determinism which denies the particular nature of man and treats him as existing solely within the framework of the natural order or by trying to behave as if the natural order had no 'givenness' and was capable of endless modification by man to suit his desires. The second complicating factor is that in the past the 'givenness' of the natural order was regarded improperly as applying to human situations which can and should be changed, such as the rigid ordering of human society in a caste system.

Man must learn to distinguish between those things which are given and which he must accept as part of his creatureliness, and those conditions which, exercising his responsibility towards creation, he must seek to change. This task of discernment has become more acute as a result of the scope of modern technology. It is, however, a responsibility which must be accepted. As Philip Sherrard has pointed out forcibly:

One of the most vicious fallacies—and one particularly rife

within the Christian world—is that it is possible for man to realize his spiritual destiny while by-passing or ignoring the complexities of his existence as a created being. If he cannot know and accept and nourish the basic realities of his created existence, his spirituality, however lofty and convincing it may appear, will be fundamentally false and hollow.[17]

Whatever the factors which have led to the shift of attitude or encouraged it, it presents an acute problem to Christians in proclaiming the gospel. The fundamental reason for the shift lies in the fact that an ontological outlook to life carries with it the recognition of dependence. It means accepting that, while a human being is free to choose, he is not a wholly autonomous being. His freedom has to be exercised within a given framework, whether it be his genetical make-up or his unavoidable dependence upon society and other human beings. The reflection of dependence raises serious enough problems in thinking about God and the relationship of man and creation to God. It becomes acute when the gospel is considered, for the gospel demands that we think ontologically if we are to understand the love and grace of God. At the heart of the gospel is the fact that our reconciliation to God and our union with him are the result of the action of his free unmerited love. The great phrases of the New Testament, 'sanctified in Christ Jesus', 'member of Christ', 'with Christ in God', 'new creatures in Christ', must be understood ontologically if the gospel is not to be stood on its head and the status of a Christian regarded as the result of his efforts. Thinking ontologically means accepting the reality and effect of love. It means accepting that love gives a person his worth and that if a person is loved he is not the same as if he were not, even though he may reject that love. The Christian life is pre-eminently the response of man to God in which he exercises his freedom to live out the meaning of what he has become by the loving and creative action of God. It was Dietrich Bonhoeffer who

16

pointed out that in the New Testament Christians are described by the use of the passive tense. 'Baptism', he wrote, 'is essentially passive—*being baptized, suffering* the call of Christ. In baptism man becomes Christ's own possession . . . He is wrested from the dominion of the world and passes into the ownership of Christ.' [18]

The present emphasis on 'doing' rather than 'being' not only leads to difficulties in communicating the gospel. It also leads to an unwillingness to accept the contingent nature of life, even Christian life, on earth and to a desire to find absolute security in the temporal. The Church forgets that

> she stands between two worlds, a world dying and a world struggling to be reborn; her life is on earth, her citizenship is in heaven. By faith she is known as the spotless bride of Christ; yet while the present age still runs its course her road remains the *via crucis*, her garments, humility and penitence, her watchword *semper reformandum* . . . In faith and hope we live in the mystery and the agony of the 'having' and the 'not having' and within our mortal members the powers of this age and of the age to come fight for the mastery. The Church, the body of Christ, still sinful, still encumbered with 'the body of this death', still hears the summons 'become what you are'.[19]

The second fundamental difference between the assumptions of the Corinthian Christians and those of today lies in the fact that, whereas the Corinthian may have been mistaken in his understanding of the way in which salvation was attained and of its implications for this life, he did see it in terms of union with God and of eternal significance. It is not an exaggeration to say that the average Christian today sees religion primarily in terms of the help which God can give him or her in this world, with a vague expectation for the world to come, rather than as an active and creative relationship with God; a relationship which has professional implications for this life but which is fulfilled in eternity.

To put it crudely, it is an attitude which regards God in

17

terms of his usefulness rather than as the object of adoration and love. An example of this attitude—admittedly a somewhat extreme one—is to be found in the prayer of John Ward, once M.P. for Weymouth:

> Oh Lord, Thou knowest that I have lately purchased an estate in fee simple in Essex. I beseech Thee to preserve the two counties of Middlesex and Essex from fire and earthquakes; and as I have also a mortgage at Hertfordshire, I beg of Thee also to have an eye of compassion on that county, and for the rest of the counties, Thou may deal with them as Thou art pleased. Oh Lord, enable the bank to answer all their bills and make all my debtors good men, give a prosperous voyage and safe return to the *Mermaid* sloop, because I have not insured it, and because Thou hast said, 'The days of the wicked are but short', I trust in Thee that Thou wilt not forget Thy promise, as I have an estate in reversion, which will be mine on the death of the profligate young man, Sir J. L . . . g. Keep my friends from sinking, preserve me from thieves and housebreakers, and make all my servants so honest and faithful that they may always attend to my interest and never cheat me out of my property night or day.[20]

This is, as has been said, a somewhat extreme example but there is sufficient likeness to the present-day attitude to make us uncomfortable. Such an outlook does of course lead to the attitude towards discipline and sacrifice of which I have already spoken. But there is a significant difference. The Corinthian Christian was concerned with an eternal destiny, whereas John Ward was clearly concerned with having a more comfortable time here on earth. Anyone who sought to apply theology pastorally to him would first have had to try and get him to appreciate the purpose of the gospel.

Such an approach affects, of course, the image which the Church presents to the world. Just as important is the ex-

pectation which the Church has of the world. In the words
of T. S. Eliot:

> Why should men love the Church? Why should they love
>   her laws?
> She tells them of Life and Death, and of all they would
>   forget.
> She is tender where they would be hard, and hard where
>   they like to be soft.
> She tells them of Evil and Sin, and other unpleasant
>   facts.
> They constantly try to escape
> From the darkness outside and within
> By dreaming of systems so perfect that no one will need
>   to be good.
> But the man that is will shadow
> The man that pretends to be.
> And the Son of Man was not crucified once for all,
> The blood of the martyrs was not shed once for all,
> The lives of the Saints not given once for all:
> But the Son of Man is crucified always
> And there shall be Martyrs and Saints.[21]

Why should men love the Church? Why indeed, but the
irony is that, though men reject the Church when she is true
to herself, they despise her when she is conformed to the
world.

The Church today, having lost her nerve, shows at times
an almost pathetic desire to be loved by the world. So she
too is happy to forget life and death with the world and seek
for systems so perfect that no one will need to be good. She
is hard where the world is hard and soft where the world is
soft. But it is only too evident that the world no more loves
a Church which seeks to or allows herself to be conformed
to the world than a Church which has the qualities which
T. S. Eliot describes.

How is the Church to recover her nerve and be true to
her nature? It will not be achieved by an other-worldly

19

escapism or by a spirituality which ignores the 'infection of nature [which] doth remain, yea in them that are regenerated'.[22] An other-worldly escapism cannot be true to a gospel which is rooted in the incarnation. The recovery of nerve demands the recovery of the eternal dimension, for that incarnation did not involve the conversion of Godhead into flesh but the taking of manhood into God. It will involve recognizing the secularism of the age in which the disciples of the incarnate Lord now live.

As Professor McGill has said,

Modernity—with its sense of God's absence and its struggle against the enormous weight of the world—turned out not to be a viewpoint or an interpretation that man 'adopted' by some will of his own and that he could drop whenever he saw fit. It proved to be an enveloping atmosphere in which he lived. He could no more leave it at will than jump out of his own skin.[23]

If we believe that human life in its totality was taken into God through the incarnation, then the secularism of today is but one aspect of it. The Christian has a right to expect of his pastors guidance as to how he can live an authentic Christian life in the present situation and how human life in a secular situation is to be redeemed. It is largely because such guidance is not given that so many of us Christians, while not being particularly sinful, are not significantly different from those who make no profession of belief in that we do not manifest recognizably God-like qualities.

The most urgent need for the pastoral theologian today is to examine the nature of that atmosphere in which we live so that we may discern both the pressures which are continually upon us and the qualities which should distinguish a truly authentic Christian life.

20

CHAPTER 2

The purpose of pastoral theology is so to apply the gospel that men and women are enabled to grow in union with God by transformation into the likeness of Christ. Such growth has to take place in this world of space and time, though it will be fulfilled in eternity. It is impossible for us to escape the world of which we are part even if we go into the desert. Indeed, the preoccupations of the world may anaesthetize us to its real problems, and it can be that in the desert we become most conscious of reality. But more: God, with whom we are to grow in union, is God who has identified himself with the world which he has created. To grow in union with God must also mean understanding the world and learning to love him through it, not in spite of it. The very structure and order of the world and its predictability gives us the sphere and framework in which we are enabled to exercise the freedom which is the source of our ability as human beings to love God and one another. It also means that we have to live in a world which is distorted and corrupted by men's misuse of that freedom.

If, therefore, our pastoral theology is to be effective and fruitful, we must take account of the actual situation in which we are to live as Christians as well as of the content of the gospel. It follows from the gospel that we should do so. To say that God loves us can be understood as meaning that we do not have to earn his love, and that is true. It also means that God loves us as we actually are at this moment, in this place. He loves us as we exist in all the complexities and ambiguities of human life which arise from the natural order, from society, and from within ourselves. What God wills for us as the expression of his love does not apply to a hypothetical situation. It applies to us as we are. Pastoral theology, which is concerned to enable men and women to love God by doing his will, must take account of the situation in which they live. So we must consider the nature of the atmosphere in which Christians live in this country today. Only by taking account of it can we discern the pressures upon them to be conformed to this world and help them to discern the will of God and do it. Before considering that atmosphere, three preliminary points must be made.

First, it is the atmosphere in Britain and not in the world which will be considered. Some of what follows applies elsewhere but if we were considering the atmosphere in which Christians lived in for example the USSR, the USA or Kenya there would be significant differences.

Secondly, while being realistic about the situation, it is necessary to keep a sense of proportion. In his admirable apologia for his Christian faith, William Rees-Mogg, the editor of *The Times*, writes:

In what period and in what place can a real age of faith be located? So far as my reading of history goes, there has always been a pious minority, and they have always been a minority. The majority have always been decent folk, ordinary people of kindly dispositions, but not very religious. There has also always been a minority of evil men who have always hated God and religion and worshipped power, and have sometimes through winning power been able to control the lives of whole nations. This is the pattern even of our present age of unfaith, though undoubtedly the non-religious majority are more remote from religion than they have normally been in the past, and the evil men are, or in the earlier twentieth century have been, unusually prominent and powerful.[1]

We make a great mistake if we base our pastoral theology on the assumption that the ordinary man is deliberately and positively wicked. It is difficult to assess the attitude of the average man or woman to religion. It is true, of course, that only a minority are sufficiently committed in their beliefs to worship God regularly and in public, though it is significant that, as a corporate activity, the percentage of people attending church regularly compares favourably with the percentage attending football matches regularly. Nevertheless polls indicate from time to time that, while the majority of our contemporaries may have little, if any, *active* interest in religion, it is a minority who are positively anti-religious. Further, anyone engaged in the pastoral ministry will be well aware of the extent to which people look for a religious solution when faced with personal disaster. (Among the problems facing pastors today are those of how to provide guidance and help in such situations without giving the impression of capitalizing on the person's misery, and of how to do so when guidance and help may be understood on the wrong term as seeking to make use of God.) Again, account must be taken of the work of the Religious Experience Research Unit and of the evidence of a wide range of admitted religious experience. On the other hand, simply to say, as Mr Rees-Mogg does, that the non-religious majority are more remote from religion than they have normally been in the past does not adequately express the fact that religion has become more remote publicly whatever the situation in the private sphere. It is hard to deny that a general sense of the irrelevance of religion is much more evident than in the past. We live in a secular atmosphere, and even when moral issues are raised, their connection with religion, even for believers, is seldom recognized or expressed. This may in part be due to the fact that we live in an increasingly multi-cultural and multi-racial society, as a result of which moral issues are presented in ways which are likely to appeal to the majority of whatever faith or of no faith, but it also reflects the current sense of the public irrelevance of religion,

23

which is regarded as an idiosyncratic activity of a few. One effect of this is to make it much more difficult for the committed Christian to be unselfconscious about his faith and its practice. The general sense of the irrelevance of religion has been fostered, particularly since the war, by those who might be described as pseudo-intellectuals. That description would seem to be apt and justified because it applies to those who do not pursue truth objectively for its own sake but are committed to value-judgements on emotional or ideological grounds and regard truth as subordinate to them. They seek by the skilful use of modern scientific and technological terms or modern discoveries in, say, archaeology to give the impression that such value-judgements particularly with regard to morality and religion are demanded by modern knowledge.[2] In one sense there is nothing new in this. Professor Owen Chadwick has said of the Press in the nineteenth century that

> in framing opinion, it impassioned it. The growing mass of the people which read newspapers could follow politics only in outline . . . they did not desire news about Parliament or foreign policy. They looked instead for symbols of the political struggle, for broad schemes, for attitudes, which were articulated less by news than by slogans. The citizen who newly became political wanted to take sides. He wished his opinion confirmed, supported, and made emotional. The new reader liked the chance of being emotional for his cause. Moral indignation became the simplest expression of an articulated viewpoint towards politics or society.[3]

Clearly, the opportunities are now much greater, especially on television, but the significant difference is that, whereas in the nineteenth-century Press it was evident that there was a battle for a cause, the effect of the pseudo-intellectual is to undermine the beliefs of a reader or viewer and win him to one side without his being aware of the process.

One most obvious characteristic of the present atmosphere

24

is the desire for immediate results. Another way of putting it would be to say that there is an impatience with time as necessary for growth.

In the last chapter reference was made to the contemporary search for happiness based on the satisfaction of immediate desires rather than the attainment of excellence through discipline and sacrifice. Dorothee Soelle has spoken of the desire to be in God's image without attaining Christ's image as a 'desire for immediacy which wants everything without detour and without self-actualization'.[4] But that is to speak of the most significant expression of this characteristic. The important point is that such desire for immediate results is evident throughout modern life. Whether it is present at the lower levels because it is present at the top and has percolated down or whether its presence at the top is the result of its being experienced lower down is a matter for debate. What matters for our purpose is that it is a characteristic of life at all levels.

A great number of advertisements offer a solution to a problem or the attainment of a desirable goal simply by the purchase of the product advertised and without other effort on the part of the purchaser. It may at first sight seem rather trivial to begin with advertisements but the effect of them is very considerable. Manufacturers would not be prepared to spend such vast sums on advertising if that were not the case. No one who has read or seen anything about the subliminal effects of advertising can be left in any doubt about the impression it makes. They may well be left very disturbed when they realize how their beliefs and judgements about values can be modified subconsciously. With regard to the way it affects people's ability to hear the gospel, two points have to be made. The first is the obvious one that it inevitably puts a premium upon the value of material objects as satisfying human desires. It does this by suggesting not only that a material object itself can be wholly satisfying, but also that certain human desires are important and ought to be satisfied. We do not see advertisements for fidelity or

25

honesty, which is understandable as these are not products for sale. Nor do we see advertisements advocating products which, it is alleged, will enable us to achieve these qualities. That is as it should be. It is disturbing to see some advertisements for religion which are in fact wholly secular in that they appear to offer religion for the wrong reasons and to suggest that its benefits can be acquired at no cost. Secondly, advertisements sometimes suggest that material objects can produce qualities which make us attractive and desirable to others without any change in our personal attitudes. The same kind of attitude is seen in those advertisements which suggest that we can acquire a skill, such as speaking a foreign language or playing a musical instrument, in a matter of weeks or months without the need for arduous practice. The influence of violence on television is much debated, particularly as its effect on crimes of violence may be greater than is often alleged. Where it may have a more fundamental effect is in implying that everyone has a right to what they want, to expect to get it without delay, and to demand it by force if it is not forthcoming. It is the combination of a desire for immediate results with the acceptance of a degree of force as normal which is so potent. Inflation reinforces the desire for the immediate, and has a powerful effect in discounting the value of the long-term view. The insistence on immediate comment by those engaged in situations of conflict has the effect of minimizing the importance which is given to reflection and patience in personal relationships. One result of this desire for immediate results is a refusal to face problems which do not appear to be capable of immediate solution.

Such a desire is contrary to the way of nature. The universe has taken millions of years to evolve. Plants and animals develop through processes of growth and adaptation which take time. It might have been expected that the general acceptance of evolution would have led people to take the long-term view more than in the past. Certainly the immediate effect of the acceptance of evolution was the optimistic liberal view that the world was gradually getting

26

better and better. This has been shattered by two world wars and the period between them, but strangely has been replaced, not, as might have been expected, by a long-term view based on struggle and adaptation but by the desire for immediacy and in some quarters a determination to maintain the *status quo*.

However, the real problem lies in the fact that a desire for immediacy is incompatible with the development of spiritual or moral goodness. Canon Roger Lloyd made this point with great force in his book *The Mastery of Evil* nearly forty years ago at a time when people were far more conscious of the power of evil than they are today:

. . . evil has an initial advantage over good in that it makes the easier and swifter appeal to that which governs the human will. 'I could be good if I would', said St Augustine, 'but I won't. Who will make me?' What does govern the human will? Certainly not the intellect, for the intellect by itself sets nothing in motion. Nor emotion itself, for emotion is more fluctuating than purposeful. The real governor of the will is imagination. What we call will-power is really imagination-power; and the prodigies which the undivided will and the single mind of a Napoleon or a Hitler have achieved have really been due to their ability to hold one picture, and only one, steadily before their mind's eye. They gaze and gaze upon it and their will is summoned and their sinews stiffened. It is not possible to find a much deeper layer in human consciousness than the imagination, for it is a completely spiritual entity, to which both evil and good, by virtue of the spiritual reality which resides in them, are able to make their appeal. But in this, evil has far the easier task. There is always a strong element of disciplined austerity in the pictures which good presents to our imagination, whereas those of evil are swiftly and immediately attractive. The rewards of an evil act are paid at once and on the spot, whereas the transactions of good are generally on a long credit basis. It is the difference

27

between lust and love. Anyone can lust; it is the easiest thing in the world, and its rewards are both pleasurable and immediate. Love, too, presents a haunting image to the imagination; but love, being a settled disposition of the mind, can give its rewards only to a mind steadily disciplined and purged. So it is with the difference between power for power's sake, which is evil, and power for service's sake, which is good. Anyone can desire the first, but to desire the second is possible only to a mind already trained to look upon the things that are excellent.[5]

To grow in love and goodness requires that we take the long-term view, whereas today the emphasis is on quick results. It is significant that the 'works of the flesh' which St Paul lists in the letter to the Galatians are all actions or activities which bring immediate and short-lived satisfaction, whereas the fruits of the spirit are qualities which demand time for their manifestation and growth.[6] The desire to achieve satisfaction without cost is closely related to another feature of the present moral climate: the refusal of people to accept responsibility for their actions. Great stress has been laid in recent times upon the freedom and rights of the individual and no Christian should want to question this. One of the fundamental truths revealed in the cross is that God has chosen to redeem us in a way which respects human freedom and still leaves man free to choose whether to respond or not to the love of God. But that freedom must be exercised with responsibility and with a willingness to accept the consequences of one's actions and decisions. The popular attitude today is that a person must be free to do what he wants, but that he must at the same time be freed from the consequences. Recently a well-known figure who has been twice divorced spoke of his campaign to secure justice for those men who, having divorced their wives, found themselves required to maintain two wives when the former wife chose not or was not in a position to marry again. It did not seem to have entered his head that having exercised his freedom to marry and then divorce his wife he was morally obliged to face the consequences. The use of the word 'justice' to describe action designed to detach the consequences of an action freely taken from the action itself is to distort the concept of justice. Justice, if it is to be true and fair, requires that a person live with the logical and proper consequences of his actions, neither evading them nor having to accept more than is attributable to them. When mercy tempers justice, it must, if the person concerned is to be treated truly as a human being, be seen as mercy as forgiving the action and its consequences. It must not be seen as condonation which denies human responsibility for action or separates the consequences from the action. In the matter of abortion, the advocates of the present position, or of an even more libertarian one, frequently present the issue as a choice between the alternatives of legalized abortion or an increase in back-street abortions. Seldom, if ever, is it suggested that the right way would be to remove the need for abortions by responsibility in sexual intercourse, whether by abstinence or the use of contraceptives (to which those who advocate abortion cannot be expected to have moral objections). If such responsibility is not exercised and a child is conceived, it is assumed that those who have so acted have a right to be relieved of the consequences of their action. Those who adopt such an attitude but have also something of a conscience about the morality of their actions will often seek to justify them. They demand that, because they have felt free so to act, the Church should then declare that what they have done is morally good. From this it is then argued that though their action had unfortunate results it is morally right, even required, that they should be relieved of the consequences. So it has been argued by a couple that living together was morally right, because they loved each other, but that when a child was conceived it should be aborted, since there was no prospect of a permanent home.

Newman laid great stress upon the importance of conscience as characteristic of human beings. He believed that

29

it played a great part in our knowledge and understanding of God, going so far as to say that 'were it not for this voice, speaking so clearly in my conscience and my heart, I should be an atheist, or a pantheist, or a polytheist, when I look in to the world.' On the other hand, he was also well aware of how it can be corrupted and wrote: 'Conscience is a stern monitor, but in this century it has been superseded by a counterfeit, which the eighteen centuries prior to it never heard of, and could not have mistaken for it, if they had. It is the right of self-will.' [7]

In public affairs the situation is somewhat different. It is not so much a question of the exercise of the individual's right with the expectation that someone else will deal with the consequences, as of a minimizing of personal responsibility. It is comparatively rare for those in public positions to accept such responsibility for their actions. How often does one hear someone say that they have made a mistake; an error of judgement perhaps, but an admitted mistake? It may well be that the increasing tendency to litigate or seek compensation has an inhibiting effect on such admissions, but the fact remains that such is the case. There has been a steady reduction in the extent to which it is accepted that there is a moral element in public affairs, except in certain sharply defined areas such as race relations. The impression is often given that those in positions of responsibility are manipulators seeking to control as skilfully as possible impersonal forces over which there is no real control, rather than that they are engaged in a situation in which they have to make decisions for good or ill.

It is ironical that, while personal responsibility is in decline, moral indignation is on the increase. It is ironical because to be morally indignant about another person or a group is to assume that they are responsible and are capable of mending their ways. The explanation may well be that moral indignation today often springs from commitment to an ideological standpoint, rather than from a belief in the capacity and willingness of human nature to respond to a moral challenge. This would account for the strangely selective way in which moral indignation is exercised.

We live among people with a selective conscience, people who no longer judge on generally acknowledged grounds of right and wrong, but consciously or unconsciously make heroes of those whom one political group or another find ideologically acceptable and allow no merit at all to the miscreants on the other side of the fence. The rulers of Chile, Spain or South Africa are detestable to some; those of the Soviet Union, Cuba or Czechoslovakia are no less detestable to others. The outraged denouncers of torture in Chile and Brazil keep silent, or even find excuses, when torture no less vile is used in Eastern Europe.[8]

Another characteristic of the mental climate in which we live is the attitude to evil. It would perhaps be better to speak of sin, for evil, if it is contemplated by the ordinary person, is usually thought of as an impersonal force on a cosmic or world scale. The average man or woman seems to be able to blank this off from his or her consciousness. Many in this country will respond to an appeal to meet an urgent need many miles away as, for example, in the recent Blue Peter appeal for Kampuchea, but it is doubtful if very many of those who give pause to reflect on the reasons for that need or think of it in terms of the malevolent forces at work in the world. As William Rees-Mogg has written,

Both Britain and the United States have become very sentimental countries, countries in which there has been a separation between acts and consequences, both in doing good and in doing evil. This is the age of the long-distance giver and the long-distance killer, of the man who gives on a tax-deductible basis, and the killer who gives an order to fire a weapon that will maim or kill someone not even his subordinate will ever see.[9]

The Church is not exempt from this charge. We express our love and concern for our fellow-Christians on the other side

31

of the world or in other churches, but remain cheerfully indifferent to the needs of those in our own parishes or congregations. The evil I am speaking about is that which is within ourselves and which is for ever knocking on our door. 'Humanity', says Roger Lloyd, 'left to itself and dependent upon no resources other than its own has a deadly aptitude for dirtying all it touches. To forget this is mere pride and pride brings no blessing.' [10] There is no plan, no form of administration, no legislation, no social reform which can save us in spite of ourselves, for every plan, all administration, all legislation and all reform has to be implemented by fallible and sinful human beings in whom evil can find a response. And no amount of planning or legislation can *make* us good. At best it can only make it harder for us to be bad and easier for us to be good. The atmosphere in which we live is one in which the reality of original sin is denied and in which solutions for our problems are looked for not within but outside ourselves. To quote T. S. Eliot again:

> They constantly try to escape
> From the darkness outside and within
> By dreaming of systems so perfect
>   that no one will need to be good. [11]

Perhaps there are really only two fundamental Christian dogmas: that of the Blessed Trinity and that of original sin. The first expresses the reality of God, and the second the reality of man.

Speaking of the Blessed Trinity leads to the last quality of the present atmosphere to be considered. The revelation of God as the Blessed Trinity tells us that within his eternal Being there is a diversity in unity of love. This diversity in unity is reflected in the structure and pattern of the created universe. At the lower levels it is a diversity which operates in unity by the proper functioning of the various elements, each fulfilling its own role for the good of the whole. If you take a cross-section of a healthy living organ, you will find a structured pattern of differentiated cells or tissues. Its healthy operation depends upon the proper operation of that diversity. But if you take a cross-section through a cancerous growth, you will find a multiplicity of identical cells, one cell having begun to reproduce its identical self at the expense of the whole organ.

In its perfected form, this diversity manifested itself in human life by love. It is this of which St Paul speaks in Chapter 12 of 1 Corinthians and from which he moves into the great description of love in Chapter 13. He speaks both of the human body and of the Body of Christ, for the same principle operates in each:

> Just as a human body, though it is made up of many parts, is a single unit because all these parts, though many, make up one body, so it is with Christ; . . . Nor is the body to be identified with any one of its many parts. If the foot were to say 'I am not a hand and so I do not belong to the body' would that mean that it stopped being part of the body? If the ear were to say 'I am not an eye and so I do not belong to the body' would that mean that it was not part of the body? If your body was just one eye, how would you hear anything? If it was just one ear, how would you smell anything? Instead of that, God put all the separate parts into the body on purpose. If all the parts were the same, how could it be a body? As it is, the parts are many but the body is one. The eye cannot say to the feet 'I do not need you'.[12]

By contrast with this, the general assumption today is that equality must mean identity. In other words, it is assumed that, if people are to be regarded as of equal value in the community, they must be regarded as being the same and the roles which they perform in society as being in theory at least interchangeable. Differences which are so evident that they cannot be ignored, such as the difference between the sexes, are confined as far as possible to the private sphere. (This view is not to be identified with the desire to provide

33

equality of opportunity, which is wholly laudable and which is certainly necessary. On the contrary, equality of opportunity assumes the diverse nature of the body and enables each member to be able to exercise the particular role for which he is fitted. Admittedly, equality of opportunity presents another problem: that of the differing values which society gives to different functions, but that problem is not solved by trying to deny the nature of the body.)[13]

This view presents two problems for Christians. The first is the attitude towards the created universe which it represents, and the second is the moral result which it produces. In his attitude towards the created universe, which of course includes himself, man has to exercise his responsibility to understand, control and use it to the glory of God; but he will only be able to do this if he accepts that it is 'given'. He has to accept its own proper autonomy if he is to be able to exercise his responsibility properly and take his part in enabling creation to reflect the nature of its Creator rather than the acquisitiveness and self-centredness of man. It means recognizing, for example, that sexual reproduction, the basis of evolution, produces diversity within the human species whereas asexual reproduction results in the multiplication of identical beings.[14] The temptation to try and ignore the 'givenness' of the created universe in the interests of an ideology is not confined to the West. The Lysenko case in Russia was a classic example of trying to bend the observable facts of science to fit in with an ideological theory.

The second problem presented by this attitude is that by its very nature it produces the two endemic evils of today: envy and greed. Both of these are particularly destructive of society, and for two reasons. First, they are contrary to the nature of love which should be the cement of society. Secondly, they put work at a discount, and work is, or should be, the prime means by which the individual contributes to the common good. It is, however, envy which is particularly destructive of a Christian outlook, for it focuses the attention of a person upon himself and produces a discontent which

34

is far from divine. R. E. C. Browne has pointed out that 'there is no single virtue which can be pitted against envy: rather it is the whole quality of devout living which enables a man to rejoice in the good fortune, sanctity and abilities of others instead of being envious.' [15] Envy looks for the worst in others and produces a habit of cynical denigration, whereas it is a characteristic of true sanctity that it seeks and can discern what is of God in others and thereby draws forth its development.

If this brief analysis of the moral atmosphere in which Christians have to live is right, what implications should it have for our pastoral theology? First, we must enable Christians to become aware of that atmosphere and of the pressures under which we live. What has been said so far may seem to be too negative in approach and to have concentrated too much upon the depressing aspects of our society today. It is hoped that what follows will be positive, but it is vital to realize that we shall never enable people to live truly as Christians today unless we help them to take the measure of the forces which hinder them from doing so. It is very difficult, if not impossible, to preach the gospel *in vacuo.* Anyone who has had to teach knows that, however lucidly and attractively a point is made, it will not be taken unless it is related to some place in the mind of those being taught where it can find a lodging. Each of the qualities of the present atmosphere which have been described needs to be examined in the light of Christian doctrine but, if that process is undertaken without reference to the situation which makes it necessary, it is very unlikely that it will be fruitful in terms of Christian growth. In the same way, modes of spirituality which may properly be advocated are not likely to be productive of sanctity if they are not seen to relate to the conditions under which they have to be exercised. We must enable Christians to become aware of the present climate and then and only then can they be equipped to live in it.

But it will not suffice merely to deal with each of the

tendencies described above. Each of them in its own way raises two fundamental points about the nature of the Christian life which must be considered if any attempt to deal with the tendencies individually is not to be misunderstood.

The first point is that the purpose of the Christian gospel and of the Christian life is union with God. Union with God is both the end for which man exists and also the means by which he is enabled to achieve it. This needs to be said very firmly at the present time especially if, as is sometimes said, there are signs of a religious revival. It needs to be said for two reasons. The first concerns the causes of the atmosphere of the present day and the second concerns our reasons for being Christians and for proclaiming the gospel.

It is probably unrealistic and unprofitable to look for a single cause of the contemporary outlook. Nevertheless, it would seem that one factor lies behind each of the characteristics which have been described. It is the decline in belief in the world to come. Christians have contributed to this, partly by neglect and partly by failing to give proper content to it in terms of the gospel. Yet it is an integral part of the gospel. Our Lord's teaching, his death, and resurrection demand an eternal dimension to human existence. If such a dimension is ignored or denied, it is not surprising that there is a demand for immediate satisfaction, for human life can then appear as 'nasty, brutish and short'. To 'eat, drink and be merry, for tomorrow we die' does not then appear to be all that unreasonable as a philosophy of life. If the morally good is not of ultimate significance on a personal level, is there any valid reason why someone should not do what appears to give him or her the greatest happiness for the moment and try to alleviate any distressing consequences? Abstract values may suffice as justification for a minority, but they will never suffice for the majority. In any case, abstract values in themselves, isolated from an understanding of the significance of individuals, very easily lead to that dehumanizing attitude which sees this generation as no more than disposable material to be sacrificed on the altar of abstract values for the sake of generations to come. It is in the Christian understanding of God that values are related to the personal and abiding experience of union with love. If this life is all there is, and if dealing with evil inevitably means taking a long-term view, involving sacrifice, it is not surprising that man dreams of systems wherein no one will need to be good, and looks for amelioration of his condition through legislation, administration or technology. As a result, personal responsibility comes to be discounted. If this life is all there is, and human life is not seen as fulfilled by the consecration of an individual's distinctive temperament, gifts and abilities in a personal relationship to God, it is not surprising that envy has become the most prevalent of the seven deadly sins.

If this be so, it presents the Christian with a particular difficulty. In such a situation, if the gospel is proclaimed its purpose is very likely to be misunderstood. By those who are well disposed to religion, it may well be seen in terms of God's usefulness to us, whether in society or as individuals. In other words, it will be seen in terms of the present earth-centred outlook of modern man. This only leads to frustration, for if attempts are made to use the gospel to solve our problems on our own terms it does not work. Those who are hostile to religion will see it as aimed at providing sanctions for moral demands, which on their basis are unjustified and harmful or at best irrelevant.

The gospel must be proclaimed as enabling man to live in union with God; in a personal relationship given to man by God, which begins on earth but which transcends death. Like the incarnation itself, the gospel is not given so that the Godhead can be converted into flesh but that manhood be taken into God. At the same time, that personal relationship must be given content to show that it fulfils human nature and does not destroy it, and to show that man is not alienated from his true nature when he lives in union with God. He is both the natural and the supernatural end of our being.

37

This World is not Conclusion.
A Species stands beyond—
Invisible, as Music—
But positive, as Sound—
It beckons and it baffles—
Philosophy—don't know—
And through a Riddle, at the last—
Sagacity, must go—
To guess it, puzzles scholars—
To gain it, Men have borne—
Contempt of Generations
And Crucifixion, shown—
Faith slips—and laughs, and rallies—
Blushes, if any see—
Plucks at a twig of Evidence—
And asks a Vane, the way
Much Gesture, from the Pulpit—
Strong Hallelujahs roll—
Narcotics cannot still the Tooth
That nibbles at the soul—[16]

The fact of this nibbling at the soul must not be denied, but
the rest and the conclusion for which man seeks must be
shown to lie in God, not in himself apart from God. But if
he is to see that, and if he is to respond to the beckoning of
God, man must also be able to see that union with God will
give him the rest and happiness which he seeks. He must
have at least a sufficient glimpse of its beauty and glory to
be prepared to accept the demands which are inevitably laid
upon him if, responding to the love of God, he seeks the
glory. So we must try to give content to the phrase 'union
with God' and in particular show how it fulfils and does not
destroy our humanity, not least because it is the claim of the
contemporary atheist that it does just that.

The second point is that, since God is love and respects
man's freedom, living in union with him in a world in which
evil has a foothold—a bent world—must involve suffering.

Ultimately, suffering is the only way in which love can overcome evil. That being so, the place and significance of suffering in the Christian life must be considered. If this is not done then we can slip with fatal ease into attitudes towards suffering which are not compatible with the worship of God who is love. Suffering can never be regarded as good in itself or as an end in itself. For the Christian it must always be seen in the light of the love of God.

The desire to be in God's image without attaining Christ's image is a desire for immediacy which wants everything without detour and without self-actualization, a narcissistic desire of the ego to settle down in God, immortal and almighty, that doesn't find it necessary to 'let its life be crucified' and to experience the night of pain.[17]

Commenting on Dorothee Soelle's book, from which that passage comes, Dr Rowan Williams writes:

It is one of the great strengths of her study that she consistently refuses to identify the *acceptance* of pain with passivity in the face of it, a passivity which is in fact hardening and dehumanizing. The Christian meets pain in acceptance and *hope* . . . The presence of this hope is what makes us alive with 'newness of life' (Rom. 6:4), in the sharing of Christ's *risen* life. Christ's risen life is a life *free* from the threat of death and annihilation ('Christ being raised from the dead will never die again', Rom. 6:9), the 'threatenedness' that is part of the condition of human sin and distance from God. In sharing this life we share his freedom from 'threatenedness'; it is never—as is perfectly clear in all Paul's epistle—a freedom from exposure to suffering or from fear, but it is a decisive transition to that new level of existence, where *God* is the only ultimate horizon—not death nor nothingness.[18]

CHAPTER 3

In the last chapter the moral climate in which Christians have to live today was considered. Only in passing was reference made to the effect which it has upon their attitudes and outlook. That this effect has been considerable is undeniable. In the sphere of Christian behaviour, for example, it is argued that moral demands which the New Testament regards as inherent in Christian discipleship no longer apply and can be replaced by moral judgements more congenial to the attitudes of our time. By way of justification it is argued that the writers of the New Testament documents were so conditioned by the culture and society of their time that what they wrote cannot be determinative for Christians today. To question this argument is not to be guilty of obscurantism. In the first place, scholars differ as to the extent to which such conditioning took place. Secondly, the exercise of critical Christian judgement compels us to ask how far in our understanding of the New Testament documents we are conditioned by the culture and society of our time. There is no intrinsic reason why it should be given an authority which is denied to that of any one age. Certainly, the fact that Christian life springs from the incarnation demands that we take contemporary conditions and modern knowledge with the utmost seriousness and do not try to live in a world of our own creation, but it also demands that we exercise the task of Christian discernment and refuse to accept uncritically the outlook, judgement and priorities of our time.

This we are able to do only if we have a clear vision of our true destiny and of God in whom that destiny is to be fulfilled. The Scriptures record the events in which God revealed his essential nature. It is in the light of this overall revelation that individual passages have to be understood. If this is not done then we find ourselves interpreting a passage in the light of what modern man thinks God should be, if he exists. It is fatally easy to arrive at the point when, because certain behaviour is generally accepted as reasonable and permissible—even desirable—we say that if God is love he cannot be so hard as to prohibit it and require obstention from it. The notion that the dominant influence in the mind of the New Testament writers was contemporary thought rather than the guidance of the Holy Spirit provides convenient justification for our attitude. Even if all New Testament scholars achieved unanimity and demonstrated beyond question the moral demands which were integral to the gospel and binding upon those who responded to it, their acceptance would not depend upon the authority of the scholars nor even upon the authority of Scripture. It would depend upon the understanding of God which Christians had and from which their obedience springs. Such has always been the case, but it is particularly so at a time when happiness is equated with the avoidance of suffering and when anything is regarded as justified if it appears to enable suffering to be avoided. The really disturbing aspect of the lives of many of us Christians today is that we do not appear to know God as all-important. We show little evidence of our awareness of him and of our willingness to love him in obedience whatever may be the cost.

The Bible as a whole makes clear beyond question that God is the source and end of our life. But it also speaks to us of God with whom man is destined to have a relationship—a relationship which of all human activities has ultimate significance. In other words, although God is presented in his glory and transcendence, man is not required to live on earth with an unbridgeable gap between him and God.

41

Even at that period in the life of Israel when the nation was regarded as having more significance than the individual, it was the peculiar relationship which the nation had to Jahweh which was ultimate.

Throughout the Old Testament the difficulties which man experiences in achieving that relationship are not minimized. Rather, as is so evident in the Psalms, they are expressed in uncompromising ways. God is known as transcendent and worshipped in his glory, the glory which if a man sees he shall not live, at whose look the earth trembles and at whose touch the hills smoke. He is God from whom man cannot escape. 'Whither shall I go then from Thy Spirit: or whither shall I go then from Thy presence? If I climb up into heaven, Thou art there: if I go down to hell, Thou art there also.' [1] Yet He is also God to whom a man can cry 'Thou hast laid me in the lowest pit: in a place of darkness and in the deep. Thine indignation lieth hard upon me: and Thou hast vexed me with all Thy storms.' [2] He is God who is to be worshipped by the offering of a sacrifice which is to be no mere cultic rite of appeasement but an offering of thanksgiving and moral righteousness. He is God who allows the innocent to suffer and the wicked to prosper. Yet he is also known in his immanence as the Shepherd who feeds Israel in green pastures and leads them forth beside the waters of comfort. 'When Israel was a child I loved him, and I called my son out of Egypt . . . I led them with reins of kindness, with leading-strings of love. I was like someone who lifts an infant close against his cheek: stooping down to him I gave him his food.' [3]

In the fullness of time God reveals himself in Christ to be one who does not merely perform loving acts but who is Love in himself. The purpose of those acts, particularly in the life, death and resurrection of Christ, is seen to be to enable man to participate in the life of God rather than just be the passive beneficiary of love.

Blessed be the God the Father of Our Lord Jesus Christ

who has blessed us with all the spiritual blessings of heaven in Christ. Before the world was made, he chose us, chose us in Christ, to be holy and spotless and to live through love in his presence, determining that we should become his adopted sons, through Jesus Christ for his own kind purposes, to make us praise the glory of his grace, in whom, through his blood, we gain our freedom, the forgiveness of our sins.[4]

God's acts of love are not merely to enable man to live in this world in peace, security and happiness, 'each man under his vine and his figtree', but to share in the relationships of love which are revealed as existing within God himself and from which proceed his loving acts towards man. In other words, though living in a universe of space and time which is of God's creation, he is called to a supernatural destiny which transcends it. The doctrine of the Blessed Trinity developed historically as the Church sought to articulate her experience of the risen and living Christ and the gift of the Spirit in the light of her belief in the one God of Abraham, Isaac and Jacob. It is, however, implicit in the acts of God to which the documents of the New Testament bear witness. 'The Old Testament doctrine of a word of God going forth in history while remaining the word of God even within the world, already contains a dynamic concept of revelation,' writes Karl Rahner.

This concept, in the progress of the history of revelation, was 'bound' to lead to the concept of the self-communication of God which would imply the Trinity since such self-communication cannot be reduced to the status of a human word 'about' God, even as a mystery, but comes in faith in the word *of* God, sustained by God himself in grace. The personification of divine forces ordained to the world—the word, wisdom, the spirit of God—which are distinct from God and are still not intermediate powers between God and the world, are formally and materially preludes to a doctrine of the Trinity in the New Testament.

Rahner accepts that no systematic doctrine is to be found there but shows how those preludes are fulfilled in ways which led the Church to formulate the doctrine.

> When the New Testament speaks simply of 'God', it means the God who has been seen at work in the Old Testament. He is the 'Father', he has a Son, and he gives his Spirit. 'God' does not stand for the triune 'Godhead'. The statements about the Son and the Holy Spirit occur when the Son and the Spirit are spoken of in the context of salvation-history; but not within the framework of a systematic statement on the Trinity. While the New Testament authors cannot speak of Jesus as 'God', since this would be, for them, to identify Jesus and the Father, they recognize the diversity of the Son. They do not look upon the Son as a cosmic power intermediate between God and the world.

Rahner says that the latter point applies also to the Spirit and concludes 'Though they are thus the saving presence of God [the Father] himself, the Son and the Spirit are not simply identical with him whom they reveal and whose radical closeness to men they are.' [5] This is evident in the Trinitarian blessing of St Paul at the close of 2 Corinthians, 'The grace of the Lord Jesus Christ, the love of God and the fellowship of the Holy Spirit be with you all', which itself reflects many passages in the epistles where the functions of the Son and the Spirit are identified with the work of God yet not with that of the Father.

In the synoptic Gospels the three key events of the baptism of our Lord, his transfiguration, and the cross all point to God who exists in a relationship of Love. Jesus is presented as being in a living relationship, that of Sonship, to God as Father, in the Spirit who is of God.

In each of the three accounts of the baptism the order is

the same: Jesus is baptized; the heavens are opened; the Spirit descends, and the voice is heard. By submitting to the baptism of John, Jesus identifies himself with humanity in its need, a need which is then shown to be fulfilled not merely by the forgiveness of sins but by the taking of that manhood into God. 'You are my son, the Beloved.' [6] The identification, because it is an identification with man in his sinful condition, has to be consummated on the cross. His baptism involves giving his life as a ransom for many in order that men and women may share his Sonship, being adopted in him, the Beloved Son. The purpose of the baptism is made clear at the outset. The humanity of Jesus is related by the Holy Spirit in Sonship to God as Father and is taken into God. As St Gregory Nazianzen says, 'Jesus comes forth from the water, bearing the world with him and the heavens which Adam had closed to himself and his descendants are opened, as the gates of Paradise by the flaming sword.' [7] Paradise is seen to be nothing less than a participation in the life of the community of love which is God, a participation which is a sharing in the Sonship of Christ.

After the Petrine confession and the first prediction of the passion, this truth is reaffirmed in the transfiguration and it relates to both. In the light of Peter's scandalized reaction to the prospect of the passion it reaffirms that the way to the cross is the way of God, but it also reaffirms that the purpose of the passion is glory and no mere earthly liberation. The transfiguration is associated in the Synoptic Gospels with the baptism. The narrative of both reflects the Exodus narrative. 'The Spirit descending' is an allusion to Isaiah 63:11, where Moses, the shepherd of the flock, is described as endowed with the holy spirit of Jahweh to bring the people through the sea. The dove was a symbol of Israel in the Old Testament, and in rabbinical commentaries 'Jesus is thus designated as the representative of God's new people according to the Spirit.' [8] A significant difference between the old and the new exodus is evident in the words of Peter at the transfiguration. Whereas there was a need for tents during

45

the journey in the wilderness to the promised land, the end is already present eschatologically in Christ and there is need no longer. The Kingdom of God is at hand in the person of Christ and in union with him man can live in union with God whose eternal presence is signified in the cloud. The parallel with Exodus also makes clear, as at the baptism, the corporate nature of the life of the Kingdom. As God had come down on Sinai to form his people, so the Spirit descended on Jesus that in him the people of God might be re-created. Further, as Edward Malley has pointed out, the fact that the disciples too are overshadowed by the cloud shows that, far from being mere spectators, they are deeply involved in the mystery of Christ's glorification as representatives of the new people of God.[9]

In the narrative of the passion, the references to the relationships within the Godhead are, as one might expect, more muted, for the divine love is manifested in identification with man in his alienation from God. Nevertheless, when our Lord is challenged as to his Divine Sonship he asserts it and, quoting Daniel 7:13 and Psalm 110:1, does so in terms which are unmistakably those of eschatological and transcendent glory. Further, as the passion narrative proceeds, the relationship with the Father is made evident in the divine converse in Gethsemane and in some of the words from the cross, which serve to emphasize both the depth of identification and the scandal of the 'Passion of our God', to quote the martyr Ignatius. This is particularly so in the cry of dereliction when the divine converse of Sonship is silenced and instead is heard the cry of man from the depths of his alienation.

The passion narratives both in the Synoptic Gospels and in St John are illuminated by the Johannine discourses. The discourses, particularly that in John 17, express with the utmost delicacy and sensitivity the relationship between the Father, the Son and the Spirit as the passion proceeds from their mutual love. 'I call you friends, because I have made known to you everything I have learned from the Father.'[10]

46

But when the Spirit of truth comes he will lead you to the complete truth, since he will not be speaking as from himself but will say only what he has learnt; and he will tell you of things to come. He will glorify me since all he tells you will be taken from what is mine. Everything that the Father has is mine; that is why I said: 'All he tells you will be taken from what is mine.' [11]

May they all be one, Father, may they be one in us, as you are in me and I am in you, so that the world may believe it was you who sent me. [12]

I have made your name known to them and will continue to make it known, so that the love with which you loved me may be in them, and so that I may be in them. [13]

Turning to Paul, it is difficult to exaggerate the emphasis which he places upon the fact that in Christ we are united to God. 'You are, all of you, sons of God through faith in Jesus Christ,' he says to the Galatians, 'all baptized in Christ, you have all clothed yourselves in Christ.' [14]

God sent His Son, born of a woman, born to be a subject of the Law, to redeem the subjects of the Law and to enable us to be adopted as sons. The proof that you are sons is that God has sent the Spirit of His Son into our hearts: the Spirit that cries, 'Abba, Father', and it is this that makes you a son, you are not a slave any more; and if God has made you son, then He has made you heir. [15]

In the letters to Corinth, the emphasis is more on union with Christ, but he is spoken of as the 'image of God' [16] and the relationship between the believer and Christ is spelt out in terms of his relationship with God, who has reconciled the world to himself in Christ. It is 'in Christ' that St Paul was caught up into Paradise. [17]

At the same time St Paul is also concerned to emphasize, particularly of course to Corinth, the corporate nature of life with Christ in God. He does so in terms both of the body and of Adam. Of that life love must be the chief quality. As the love of God was seen in the death and resurrection of Christ, so the love of Christians is to be seen in their death to life, dying to all that separates them from God and their neighbours to live the new life centred in Christ and the brethren. So he recalls the Christians in Rome to the meaning of their baptism.

> You have been taught that when we were baptized into Christ Jesus we were baptized in his death; in other words, when we were baptized we went into the tomb with him and joined him in death so that as Christ was raised from the dead by the Father's glory, we, too, might live a new life . . . That is why you must not let sin reign in your mortal bodies.[18]

Just as St Paul constantly emphasizes that the acts of God in Christ for our salvation spring from his love for us, so he emphasizes the lovelessness of sin both in terms of our response to God and in terms of our love for the brethren and for our neighbours.

It is, of course, St John who speaks most explicitly of love; both the love of God and love for the brethren. But what is often overlooked is that what he says is in the context of our union with God. 'What we have seen and heard we are telling you so that you may be in union with us, as we are in union with the Father and with his Son, Jesus Christ.' [19] While stressing the love which we must have for God and for one another, he repeatedly speaks of it in terms of the life of God himself with whom we are to live in union, just as when speaking of light and darkness he says 'God is light; in Him is no darkness at all. If we say that we are in union with God while we are living in darkness, we are lying because we are not living the truth.' [20] So we read 'God is Love and anyone who loves lives in God and God lives in Him.' [21] Like St Paul, St John, by way of testimony, recalls us to the gift of the Spirit, by whom we are able to discern and embody the qualities which are of God, and the water of baptism and the blood of the Eucharist, by which we are enabled to experience the death and resurrection which must be at the heart of every Christian's life if he is to do the truth.

The Christian is called to nothing less than to share in the life of love which is God himself, the Blessed Trinity, who not only creates men and women but draws them by the love which he is into union with himself. Because it is a life of fellowship with the Blessed Trinity, so the life of the Christian is Trinitarian. Through Christ, by the power of the Spirit, he is enabled to be caught up, as it were, into the love of the glory of the Father. In the Word made flesh, the relationship of love in the Blessed Trinity was uttered within creation (which itself springs from that love). In Christ our humanity glorifies the Father in love through the Spirit. The Christian is called to share in that consecration of human life to the glory of the Father in love. He is called to share in the eternal movement of love which flows from the love of the Godhead through creation in Christ to God. It is, therefore, quite inadequate to think of the Christian life as no more than ordinary life in time assisted by God, albeit with the expectation that it will be followed by life in the world to come. Nor is it adequate to see it as a spiritual life to be pursued independently of, or even in spite of, ordinary life. Yet, as Karl Rahner has written, 'despite their orthodox confession of the Trinity, Christians are, in their practical life almost mere "monotheists". We must admit that should the doctrine of the Trinity have to be dropped as false, the major part of religious literature could well remain unchanged.' [22] By contrast, as Fr George A. Maloney, S. J., has written 'In the earlier centuries of Christianity theology was a mysticism about the indwelling Trinity, living within and transforming Christians into divinized children of God.' [23] The Christian life is a life of union with God the Blessed Trinity, sharing his creative, redemptive and sanctifying love.

As was mentioned earlier, the Christian life is essentially

49

supernatural; it is also natural in the sense that man is created for union with God and that to love and serve God fulfils his true self. We must, therefore, examine how human love is related to and fulfilled in the love of God.

It will be very obvious to those who know Martin D'Arcy's great book *The Mind and Heart of Love*, first published in 1945, that the analysis which follows is deeply indebted to it. It is not suggested that it adequately reflects the profundity and range of his thought, but it is hoped that it does reflect the all-embracing way in which the various expressions of human life are consecrated in the love of God. His approach is compelling because of its coherence and basic simplicity. It takes account of the structures and operation of the physical universe. It looks with understanding at the diverse ways in space and time through which man has sought to discover and fulfil the purpose of his existence. The psychological element in human behaviour is recognized. It deals with the perennial problem of Eros and Agape in a way which neither denies the possibility of the redemption of Eros nor undermines the divine initiative and the priority of grace represented by Agape. In considering the question of disinterested love and self-love it does not attempt to cut the Gordian knot by maintaining that the one is good and the other evil: a way which refuses to recognize that love of self is included in our Lord's Summary of the Law. Above all, it allows the doctrines of the Blessed Trinity and the incarnation to illuminate human experience in a most fruitful way.

From time immemorial man has sought to answer the riddle of the universe and discover its meaning and direction. Some have attempted to do so in terms of a harmonizing principle or philosophy which co-ordinates and directs. Others have sought to find it in what is called the law of opposites—the everlasting rhythm of birth and decay, of being and becoming, of winter and spring, of love and hate. Long before Hegel it was sought in a dialectic. Aristotle lists a table of opposites and gives the notions of determinants and

50

determinables of matter and form. In music, literature and science with major and minor chords, the rise and fall of accent, energy and inertia the dialectic can be seen.

This desire for truth, unity, the absolute—whatever term is used—is Eros or human desire. The word is familiar nowadays not merely through the ancient Greek legends but through the work of such scholars as Nygren,[24] de Rougemont[25] and Martin D'Arcy,[26] who have sought to relate it to Agape or divine love. Nygren sought to include all love or desire proceeding from man within Eros, which he proclaimed as wholly un-Christian and as coming under the condemnation of justification by works. Agape or divine love according to Nygren is uncaused and unmerited, bearing no relation to the deserts or efforts of human beings, producing in them a response which is also given, a response which is free of the self-centredness of any human aspirations, however noble and high-minded.

De Rougemont brings out the truth that man has a love which does not end with himself. Such a love has a habit of revolting against reason and rushing off to lose the self in some trance or ecstasy to practise self-immolation in dark mysterious rites. De Rougemont identifies this romantic love with Eros and traces its origins to Celtic rites, which expressed themselves in Christendom unbaptized in the later heresies of Manichaeism and Catharism. But as D'Arcy says, his explanation cannot be accepted. In the first place

> he does not explain how the passion of Eros can be transformed into Agape: and yet some such transformation must take place if the 'passionate' language of many Christian mysteries belong to Agape and not to Eros . . . But a much more important difficulty is that de Rougemont allows for no kind of love in between the pagan passion of Eros and the Christian and supernatural love of charity.[27]

To those two reasons another can be added. If Eros is to be identified simply with passion, the need for the element of striving and discipline to be redeemed in Agape can be very easily overlooked. The exercise of the reason and will can be taken as essentially good and the extent to which they can be corrupted by self-centredness ignored.

So, on the one hand, Eros is identified with self-love, particularly in its more powerful instrument, human reason, and on the other hand with romantic and ecstatic love, but neither identification is adequate.

Fr D'Arcy bases his analysis on what he describes as 'Give and Take'—'the simplest statement of the law which governs what is highest and lowest in the Universe.'

> In the most elementary changes in the physical world there is gain and loss, and taking on of something and the passing on of what once was and no longer is . . .

> This principle is seen more clearly in the continuation of life. There is always a duality, of which one aspect is negative compared with the other; one gives and the other takes. The giving is a surrender and implies a certain passivity, perhaps even unto death and extinction. The desire which is felt by the two parties in this momentary or prolonged union accords with the role played. There is the whoop of triumph, the exultant mastery in the act of possession and total extinction in the being of the other. It may be that the latter desire or emotion is due to a primary urge for the species and its continuation, and since there is in the lower forms of life no true individuality in either participant, there is nothing to prevent the owner of the instinct from rushing to its joy in death. The important fact to notice is the universal fact of duality.[28]

He recognizes that within this universal duality there are important differences and stresses that it is all important to emphasize the unique status of man.

> Human love has something which animal love never has. The difference can be best expressed in saying that the higher actions of man have an intrinsic value and that man

52

has a personal dignity. This dignity implies a radical difference between human love and any lower form of love. It forbids alike the possessiveness which marks the positive male surge of animal passion and the total self-yielding of feminine ecstasy. In creatures which are swayed by animal passion the male instinct is to dominate and take, the female to yield and give. They are unhindered by any moral considerations, by mutual respect. It is sufficient that they should get what they want and that the species should be continued . . . Both are needed and together they suffice, the feminine as the love which surrenders for the sake of the other or the continuation of the species, and the male as the love which seeks its own and possesses whether it be rampant or, as we shall see later, cognitive. Now, whereas in nature these instincts go their own way, careless often of individual life, on the human level each self must grow in the taking and giving and each is a sacred life which must be respected. A new cycle begins; the two loves are present and are sublimated if the lower passion is lifted up, as it should be, to the ends of the spirit.

D'Arcy then refers to another and perhaps even more fundamental difference between animal and human love.

Every human person has these two loves within him, with one usually predominant, but the sacrificial impulse has a new direction... Within the soul is a more than human love and that is why I say that the sacrifical love has a new direction .In the equality which should exist in true human love it has not its full outlet; there is more to it than a mere equality, for it is now the expression of the secret mark of human beings, namely their creatureliness, the frail-as-gossamer hold on our nature, which we call existence or persistence in being.

In other words there is in the human a consciousness of self, of being which carries with it a consciousness of dependence.

'We are hangers on, courtiers of the Absolute;' says D'Arcy, 'we can be unmade as quickly as we are made and in that dependence is felt dimly the ultimate love of the rivulet for its source.' [29] Experience would probably make us want to qualify that last sentence and say that in such dependence the ultimate love *can* be dimly felt, for it is precisely that dependence which can produce rebellion and resentment, particularly when dependence is seen as being a 'hanger on', a 'courtier of the Absolute' rather than as the expression of an invitation to love. The 'Take' of Give and Take with its emphasis on achievement by the affirmation of the self, whether by mind, body or spirit, will always reject dependence if it has not learned and does not accept that it is but half of the self.

However, that is to anticipate. Let us see where we are. Throughout creation life is marked by this duality of giving and taking, of seeking to possess by grasping and of seeking to possess by abandonment, of life by living and life through death. The movement and development of life takes place not by a spineless synthesis of the two modes but through their complementarity and their relationship. At the animal level this may be at the expense of the individual and not necessarily simultaneous. At one moment the Take may be dominant and at another time may be wholly at the mercy of Give.

At the human level, between persons, made in the image of God, the individual is not or should not be expendable. Every human being has within him the love of taking and of giving. Both are necessary and must not be denied, but both have to be reorientated to take account of the worth and dignity of the human person. Take, whether it is exercising the power of reason, physical force or emotion to achieve its end cannot do so at the expense of another person. Give cannot surrender itself so entirely as to deny or maim its own selfhood. Equally, if Take, being the action of a human person, denies another, it denies itself and Give, if it

54

seeks to capture and possess another by its own death denies itself as a person.

It will not do, therefore, to try to identify one or the other with Christian love—to equate, as Nygren did, Eros with Take and Agape with Give, seeing Take as a grasping and a denial of the priority of grace and Give as the acceptance of it in abandonment. The truth lies in the fact that, to use D'Arcy's terms, Eros has two forms, Animus and Anima. Animus is lordly pride and self-assertiveness which takes seeking to achieve in its own strength. Anima is the desire of surrender even to absorption and self-extinction, the abandonment to passion and ecstasy. Both Animus and Anima in the fulfilment of themselves in isolation lead to death. Animus in grasping fails to find; Anima in lying down to die does not rise again. The Christian gospel gave the world Agape, Christian love, proclaiming that the object of man's desire is not hidden or distant, to be achieved by self-assertion or the extinction of self, but is love itself stretching out to give and to receive, so providing the means by which both Animus and Anima find their fulfilment. Neither is left out. Animus—the lion—still seeks for the truth but learning from Anima bows his lordly head beneath the lintel of faith, receives the grace to be apprehended by the truth, and so finds it. Anima—the unicorn—dying to self in Christ finds self alive in Christ and learning from Animus strives to become by grace what she already is. Both Animus and Anima are aspects of human love and need to be redeemed.

This is evident when we contemplate the 'primordial and perfect expression' of love in God himself. To quote D'Arcy again 'in the mutual love of the Trinity all is given without loss and all is taken without change, save that a new Person is revealed in this wondrous inter-communion Who is Love itself.'[30] Within the divine community of love there is both taking and giving, but all taking is without domination and all giving is without loss of person. The perfect mutual self-giving in love which is God himself is the source of human love and in him alone is it to be fulfilled. 'With me in them and you in me may they be so completely one that the world will realize that it was you who sent me' [31] is the prayer of our Lord before his passion.

But how is that achieved? It is the work of God, who takes the initiative. Love acts for the redemption of human love, and being love, does so by an identification which is a complete self-giving yet without loss of self. 'God was in Christ reconciling the world to Himself.' [32] That for which man seeks in his highest and most noble moments—the ability to bear the burden and experience the suffering of another person while still remaining himself, and therefore able to bear it, is effected in the act of perfect love. It is love alone which can unite the finite and the infinite, the divine and the human. That is why love is the key to Christology. [33]

The point of redemption is precisely the point at which man rebels—the point of dependence springing from his creatureliness. The cross, proclaims that dependence also springs from and leads to love. So man can see that a death to self-centredness which is a death into God is a death to rise to a life in love. For the cross also proclaims that, when we speak of 'Give and Take' rather than 'Take and Give', we are reflecting a basic truth about the relationship between finite man and infinite God. Both are necessary in our love for God but because of our creatureliness Give must come first, the giving of self wholly into the hands of love in a death which brings rebirth.

Through that rebirth, both Take and Give are redeemed and fulfilled. All that Take has, of intelligence, will, power or skill, will be exercised to the full, for Take will have discovered that the self finds and knows itself when it gives itself and forgets itself in love. Give will be fulfilled, for it will know that its intuition, that death is the way to life, is reaffirmed but it will also know that a death into passion, desire, the irrational or ecstasy is a death to death, and that only a death into God who is love has the prospect of resurrection.

What is the bearing of this upon our proclamation of the

gospel and upon our responsibility to guide those who are pastors of the flock? In the first place, it enables us to show that the purpose of the gospel is fulfilment, not alienation. Our essential humanity is not denied nor is our relationship to the physical world of which we are an integral part. Our dependence upon our fellow-men is recognized and accepted. There is no denial of our instincts, including our instinct for self-preservation with its love of self. But the blind alleys into which the mere following of those instincts will lead us and the frustration which we will suffer if we use our talents in self-assertiveness are also evident. The need for a man to have an end other than in himself if he is to rise to the exercise of his highest power—an end which abides, which is eternal—is made clear.

Secondly, that end is shown to be a participation in love, but it is love which involves movement and action, not merely a feeling which is experienced in an otherwise loveless life. This is shown to be so, albeit imperfectly, even at the purely human level. Much more is it so when we contemplate the Being of God, in whose eternal life of creative and redemptive activity we are called to share. In contemplation of this activity, the Eastern Orthodox tradition of distinguishing between the essence of God and his energies can be very valuable. 'He is outside all things according to his essence but he is in all things through his acts of power' says St Athanasius, and St Basil writes 'We know the essence through the energy. No one has ever seen the essence of God but we believe in the essence because we experience the energy.' The modern Orthodox theologian, Kallistos Ware, writes:

By the essence of God is meant his otherness, by the energies his nearness. Because God is a mystery beyond our understanding, we shall never know his essence or inner being, either in this life or in the Age to come. If we knew the divine essence, it would follow that we knew God in the same way as he knows himself; and this we cannot ever do, since he is Creator and we are created. But, while God's inner essence is for ever beyond our comprehension, his energies, grace, life and power fill the whole universe, and are directly accessible to us.

The essence, then, signifies the radical transcendence of God; the energies, his immanence and omnipresence. When Orthodox speak of the divine energies, they do not mean by this an emanation from God, an 'intermediary' between God and man, or a 'thing' or 'gift' that God bestows. On the contrary, the energies are God himself in his activity and self-manifestation. When a man knows or participates in the divine energies, he truly knows or participates in God himself, so far as this is possible for a created being.[34]

It should be added that when the Orthodox speaks about the purpose of the gospel as the 'theosis' of man, his ingodding, a word which seems to cause alarm in the West, it is always seen not only as bestowed by grace but as a participation in the divine energies and never the essence. This distinction is very valuable when we come to try and see the world in its relation to God, to discern his creative and redemptive activity and to fulfil our vocation to co-operate—to be, in St Paul's phrase, co-workers with God. We learn not to try and see God in creation in some near-pantheistic sense but to see him as the source of its being who sustains its life. We can then see how, if we are to share his love, we must co-operate in the activity of that love.

Thirdly, we are enabled to see that if it is to be true love reflecting its divine source, love must be holy, that is morally good and faithful. It must continue to the end, whatever the cost. When confronted with evil, love which is merely Take will either express itself by ways which are not of love or abandon the effort. A love which is only Give will die as love in self-pity which it may then use to try and achieve its end by blackmail. But a love which is both Take and Give, both redeemed and fulfilled in Christ, will continue to participate in the divine love. This is true of our love for God, our love for other persons and of the love which we should have for ourselves. But this brings us to the question of the part which suffering must play as we share the love of God in a sinful world.

CHAPTER 4

To live as a Christian is to live in union with God who is love. But God is not just 'there' as it were, 'waiting for Godot', waiting for man, whom he has created and redeemed, to respond to what he has done; waiting for a response which will detach man from the world. God does not exist in isolation from the world. The goodness of God perpetually embraces the world in an overflowing and ceaseless movement of love. Not only is man part of that world but, in so far as he participates in the love of God, he is called to participate in that love for the world. Love is that alone which unites the infinite and the finite. Man can only know God by loving him, not merely by an act of apprehension of the mind. But love involves movement and relationship and man cannot love God except by being caught up into the movement of the divine love. He cannot know God simply as an object of the intellect.

But the world which God loves is a 'bent' world and man, who allies himself with God who is love, is part of the 'bent' world in which he is to share in the love of God. He has to recognize the presence of evil and accept that within himself there is always that from which evil can find a response. But more: as he seeks to love he has to accept that, whenever love comes face to face with evil, love will suffer. Not to suffer is not to love. Indeed it is love which makes us see suffering as a problem. If we do not love, why should suffering trouble us? I am, of course, not merely speaking of pain. Although pain is an inseparable part of suffering, the function of pain by itself is to enable suffering to be abolished. It serves to indicate the presence of disorder or the threat of disorder. Such disorder may be in the physical realm, or, in the case of man, since he is a psychosomatic unity, it may be experienced physically but really refer to disorder in the mental or spiritual areas of his being. To try to abolish pain without also trying to deal with the disorders which produce it is ultimately the way of death. This fact can present us with a moral dilemma. While we very properly desire to alleviate pain, we may question the moral rightness of doing so if it seems very probable that it will lead to indifference towards the cause or causes. We are also faced by the moral problem caused by the fact that pain can be and is used immorally. Torture is an obvious example of this. The normal order is reversed. Pain is not seen as an indication of a disorder to be remedied. A disorder is produced which will cause pain which is used to serve the torturer's ends. While torture in the normal sense of the word is still not a characteristic of everyday life, though it would certainly appear to be on the increase, we seriously underestimate the extent to which ordinary people use the production of pain, both physical and mental, to try and get what they want. Battered babies and battered wives are more common than we like to realize and they are but the tip of the iceberg.

At first sight this situation seems surprising and illogical. One characteristic of our society which was only mentioned in passing earlier but which underlies all its characteristics like a ground bass is the attitude that suffering is the worst evil and that anything, however morally wrong, is justified if it appears to relieve suffering. In her book *Suffering* Dorothee Soelle refers to the apathy of society. She writes:

Apathy is a form of inability to suffer. It is understood as a social condition in which people are so dominated by the goal of avoiding suffering that it becomes a goal to avoid

61

human relationships and contacts altogether. In so far as the experiences of suffering, the *pathai* (Greek for the things that happen to a person, misfortunes) of life are repressed, there is a corresponding disappearance of passion for life and of the strength and intensity of its joys . . . I have in mind a society in which: a marriage that is perceived as unbearable quickly and smoothly ends in divorce; after divorce no scars remain; relationships between generations are dissolved as quickly as possible, without a struggle, without a trace; periods of mourning are 'sensibly' short; with haste the handicapped and sick are removed from the house and the dead from the mind. If changing marriage partners happens as readily as trading in an old car on a new one, then the experiences that one had in the old relationship remain unproductive. From suffering nothing is learned and nothing is to be learned. In the equilibrium of a suffering-free state the life curve flattens out completely so that even joy and happiness can no longer be experienced intensely. But more important than this consequence of apathy is the desensitization that freedom from suffering involves, the inability to perceive reality. Freedom from suffering is nothing other than a blindness that does not perceive suffering. Then the person and his circumstances are accepted as natural which even on the technological level signifies nothing but blind worship of the *status quo*: no disruptions, no involvement, no sweat.[1]

Anyone who knows Dorothee Soelle's book will have probably realized that these quotations omit her references to a class-based origin for such an attitude and to her judgement that it flourishes in a society in which a banal optimism prevails. What she says may be true of present-day Germany from which she writes. But in this country I do not think that the simple class-equation can be made, and a banal pessimism would be a more accurate description of our society, which can scarcely be described as optimistic. Neither of these points, however, affects the accuracy of her analysis of the way in which suffering is evaded.

It may seem surprising and illogical that the infliction of suffering on others to get one's own way should be on the increase at a time when suffering is regarded as the greatest evil. It should be neither, for the desire to avoid suffering oneself at all cost springs from a self-centredness and a failure to love. In a 'bent' world, in which suffering will not just go away, it means demanding that everyone else should bear the cost of suffering. The desire to avoid it leads to an insensitiveness towards the suffering of others.

This situation in which we have to commend the Christian gospel is complicated and intensified by the increased presence in the world of suffering on a massive scale of which we are constantly made aware through the media. On the one hand, it intensifies it because for many people the thought of evil on a cosmic or world scale has an anaesthetic effect, blanking off a consciousness of the reality of evil and reducing suffering to that which it is supposed can be dealt with by money, legislation or administration. On the other hand it complicates it. Although we have to relate to the people in this country, our immediate neighbours, we cannot ignore the problem of suffering on a world scale. Any approach to suffering which brings people to an awareness of its significance will, precisely because of that awareness, be judged to be inadequate if it does not include suffering on a world scale in its orbit.

Where then must we begin? There is only one point and that is our understanding and experience of love. If we speak about love we shall be speaking about God even when we do not do so explicitly or do so in religious terms. Unless we start with love, we shall soon find ourselves compounding evil. We must face the fact that to human beings compassion does not come easily. Sentimentality does. Most people when faced with the sick or the handicapped are embarrassed and embarrassment readily turns to impatience or resentment. This is evident on a comparatively trivial

63

level when we think of our attitude to our husbands or wives when they have a red nose and are sniffing with a common cold. We get cross, and it needs a conscious effort on our part to love them in that condition. On the other hand it is fatally easy, especially when we are concerned for a category of those who are suffering, to use our concern as something with which we beat others over the head. The more passionate our concern the easier it is to feel resentment or bitterness towards those who are responsible or to seek to manipulate those who do not share our passion by trying to produce feelings of guilt in them. Thus although we may do something to reduce evil in one context we add to it in another. Another reason for beginning with love is that love alone can deal with suffering in a way which respects human dignity and freedom. To try and deal with it forcibly at the expense of freedom is only to substitute one form of suffering for another. Dorothee Soelle has analysed the Book of Job in a penetrating way and shown that it is not so much an account of how man seeks to understand suffering as an explanation of how, given the problem of human suffering, which does not go away even if he tries to abolish God, he is to understand God. That the abolition of God does not help is recognized in Job's response to his wife's cry 'Curse God and die'. But successively, the roles for God of 'arbitrary tester', of the 'avenger who establishes his absolute purity by dirtying his own hands with blood', of the Lord of stars, seas and clouds, 'the mere Tremendum of Nature' to whom man must submit in passive, irrational and uncomprehending obedience, are examined and rejected. Job expresses his conviction that in the end God himself will appear as his vindicator and that if he could in the flesh but see God he would understand. To quote Dorothee Soelle again 'Job's call for the advocate, the redeemer, is to be understood only as the unanswered cry of the pre-Christian world which finds its answer in Christ.' [2]

Before considering how a Christian can and should use suffering fruitfully, mention must be made of the difference between suffering and temptation. The two are often confused but both have to be dealt with in the same creative way and are not to be faced in a passive and negative spirit. We suffer both because we are in a natural sense members one of another—'No man is an island'—and because of the effects of our own lack of holiness. We are tempted partly because of the nature of evil and partly because we are directly assailed by the powers of evil. Whereas goodness and holiness are essentially constructive, evil is destructive. Every time you or I become, by the grace of God, more the embodiment of goodness or holiness we are built up and become more real, more truly ourselves, for what is of God, perfect Reality, has taken form within us. We have not merely performed good acts; we have become better people and the better enabled to resist next time, when, precisely because we are better people, the temptation will be fiercer and more subtle. When we acquiesce in evil or pursue it, we become less truly ourselves, for evil leads to disintegration. It becomes harder to resist next time and there will be a next time, for the devil knows only too well that there is the possibility of penitence which will undo all he has achieved. Temptation and suffering, though distinct, are often confused because temptation pitches us into the battle between good and evil or, rather, makes us acutely aware at a point of conflict that there is a war on. Gethsemane involves both temptation and suffering. Resisting temptation is never just a question of making a moral decision coolly and dispassionately. It involves a struggle at the heart of our being as to which side we commit ourselves.

When we come as Christians, participating in the love of God, to face suffering and temptation, the really important thing is that we see the demand as calling us to be actively engaged in the redemptive power of love. Simply to endure suffering stoically can never be an adequate response for a Christian. It may be that it is better to endure than to acquiesce in and compound evil by expressing bitterness and resentment, but, simply because stoic endurance by itself is not the way of love, the temptations of self-righteousness and insensitivity are very great. Still less is it adequate for a Christian to try and evade suffering and give the impression that there is something fundamentally wrong with his Christian commitment if he is not enabled to live on a plateau of euphoria where the Lord provides and everything goes well for him. Such a view of the Christian life is incompatible with being a disciple of Jesus who 'leads us in our faith and brings it to perfection; for the sake of the joy which was still in the future, he endured the cross, disregarding the shamefulness of it, and from now on has taken his place at the right of God's throne.' [3]

The Christian way of dealing with suffering and evil is to practise the way of exchange. Whatever its source or cause, when we come face to face with suffering and evil, one of two things happens. It can find a response, a lodging, within us through which its effect can be intensified and extended. If, when suffering or evil comes to us, we allow it to produce bitterness, resentment, unholy indignation springing from self-righteousness or lack of charity, we have helped to disseminate its corrupting and disintegrating influence. If, however, we see our vocation as Christians to participate in the love of God, then the first thing we have to do is to allow the evil to spend its force within us and there to find no response, no lodging. 'Christ suffered for you and left an example for you to follow the way he took, he had not done anything wrong, and there had been no perjury in his mouth. He was insulted and did not retaliate with insults; when he was tortured he made no threats . . .' but the passage in 1 Peter does not stop there. Evil found no response in our Lord. 'We have one who has been tempted in every way that we are, though he is without sin.' The rejection of evil is followed by the positive act of trust: '. . . he put his trust in the righteous judge.' [4] And, we can add, it is evident in the accounts of the passion that that trust in the Father is accompanied throughout by love for those around him including those who are the instruments of the passion. 'Father, forgive them' . . . 'Woman, behold your son . . .' In union with Christ we have the vocation to live the way of exchange by which evil is not only resisted but is exchanged for that which is of God. Such a way is the expression and the fruit of our union with God in Christ by the Spirit. It is also the expression and fruit of our Christian *Koinonia*—our membership of the one Body—and of our common humanity.

Not only is the way of exchange at the heart of our vocation to love in a 'bent' world. It also affects our other attempts to work for its redemption. As I have written elsewhere,

> It is when our life as Christians is based upon the way of exchange that our activities of healing, reconciliation, teaching or bringing relief can be delivered both from the spirit of patronage and harsh condemnation and from un-kind condonation of sin. We fail in our vocation, if while feeding the hungry or housing the homeless, we pour out bitterness and resentment against those who produce the hunger or the overcrowding.[5]

If we are to live the way of exchange one thing is essential. We must ourselves be learning to live as those who are perpetually and joyfully under the mercy. We must know ourselves to be those who have been and are accepted by God as we are and are forgiven. But we must also see penitence and forgiveness not as a private gift for our enjoyment but as the means by which the overflowing love of God enables us to respond more fully to our vocation and to share in his love.

At this point I should like to give one very personal example of trying to practise this way. Some years ago, during the sixties when I was Bishop of Willesden, I was driving early in the morning to a meeting of a Deanery chapter at which I was first to celebrate the Eucharist and then address the members. Listening to the wireless in the car on the way I heard a report of the tarring and feathering of a young

woman in Northern Ireland who was supposed to have col-
laborated with the other side. The report was followed by
a recording of the inhuman sounds of those responsible as
they mocked and jeered the girl. I found surging up within
me feelings of anger and shame that human beings could
behave in such a way but I then was appalled to realize that,
besides these reactions which I believe were right and justified, I was experiencing and harbouring feelings of real bitterness and hatred towards them. This evil had found a
response in me and I was party to it. I was allowing myself
to be an instrument for it to extend its influence. I was not
even praying for those involved. I found that I was hating
not just those responsible but people in general. When I
arrived I could not celebrate the Eucharist until I had first
confessed my sin to God in the presence of the chapter and
asked for his forgiveness and theirs. It will not surprise you
to hear that, after the Eucharist, we abandoned the subject
on which I was billed to speak and talked about the way of
exchange. There was, of course, nothing unique in that experience. It is one which we share daily as we read the
newspapers or listen to the news and are exposed to accounts
of terrorism, hijacking, kidnapping, the plight of refugees
and the agony of bereavement. I think that the particular
incident has remained so vividly in my mind because never
before or since have I been so conscious of the choice before
us at the corporate level whether we are to be drawn in to
the web of evil or to share in the love of God.

We will now consider the pattern of Christian living today. There are two preliminary points to be made. First it
must be emphasized that what follows is to be understood
in terms of Christians in this country who have to live in
the kind of atmosphere which I tried to describe. The opportunity to meet Christians in many parts of the world, to
worship with them and discuss their practice of the Christian
life is very valuable. It helps us to appreciate that there is no
one completely authentic expression of Christian discipleship
which can simply be applied anywhere in the world. The

background and culture must be taken into account. The criticism that missionaries from this country applied a pattern of Christian practice and worship based on that in the English parish church in certain countries abroad without taking account of local conditions is a valid one as is still evident in some places today. We must not repeat the mistake in reverse by the uncritical adoption of the ways of Christians who have not been brought up in our culture and with our history. This applies not merely to learning from Christians in other parts of the world, but also to the recovery of unity in this country. In seeking to develop relationships between the Churches here, account must be taken of the differences in historical origins and development which have led to different ways of understanding Christian discipleship and spirituality. In my contribution to *A Critique of Eucharistic Agreement* [6] I referred to the danger of supposing that the needs for reform in eucharistic worship in the Roman Catholic Church were the same as those in the Church of England. Whereas whatever a Roman Catholic knows about the Eucharist, he knows it was a sacrifice, whatever an Anglican knows it to be he knows it to be a communion. The recovery of a right understanding of the Eucharist as sacrifice and communion demands a different emphasis in each Church. It is perhaps for this reason that an uncritical acceptance of modern Roman Catholic liturgical practice in the Church of England not infrequently leads to the understanding of the corporate nature of the sacrament being largely in terms of human fellowship.

The second preliminary point is that the necessary *basis* for Christian discipleship has not changed. It still consists in worship, the sacraments, prayer, the use of the Scriptures and penitence. We should regard with the greatest suspicion anyone who suggests that this is no longer the case, the same suspicion with which we would regard anyone who said that eating, drinking and sleeping were outdated activities for man in the last quarter of the twentieth century. That basis has remained unchanged during the age of persecution, at the time of the barbarian invasions, when the Byzantine empire was at its zenith, when Europe was rent apart by the Reformation, and in Russia both under the Tsar and under the Soviet regime. It remains the same in the secular post-Christian England of our time.

What has changed during the centuries is the form which the pattern has taken, and the relative importance which has been given to the various elements within it. These have both contributed to and have been the expression of a varying approach to the gospel as a whole. Sometimes the distinctive approach to a particular age has been the result of reaction against the contemporary culture, sometimes the result of conformity to it and usually a mixture of both.

It was, for example, in the light of his own impending martyrdom that, at the beginning of the second century, Ignatius developed his understanding of the Christian life as, in the words of Rowan Williams, 'the offer of life in the Spirit of God's Son and Servant, in communal life and sacramental fellowship—never simply a "mystery" of cultic participation, but an enduring communion of persons in society.'[7] It was in objection to 'a Christian life deprived of its tension towards the future, the *eschaton*'[8] and in the belief that what is 'useless and destructive is to imagine that enlightenment and virtue can be found by seeking for fresh stimulation'[9] that St Anthony located the Christian conflict in the desert. It was to give 'exceptionally strong expression to the Christian suspicion of conceptual neatness, of private revelation and religious experience uncontrolled by reference to the givenness of Christ's cross'[10] that St John of the Cross expounded his spirituality of death to resurrection. The emphases given by these exceptional Christians provide us with some idea of the prevailing outlook of Christians in their times. Reference was made earlier to the fact that the New Testament does not refer to success but to fruitfulness. It is for this reason that our first concern both for God's sake and for the proclamation of the gospel must be to discern in what way Christians can and should express their discipleship at any given time. The question we must ask is 'What pattern of Christian living enables us to bring forth the fruits of the Spirit?' To concentrate on what Christians do or how we should present the gospel in a way which the world can hear, without first concentrating on how Christians can become what they already are, can lead us into real trouble.

In describing the necessary emphases in Christian life today no attempt is made to put them in any order of importance. They are inextricably related to each other and dependent upon each other. No single one can be isolated as cardinal. They are all aspects of a particular awareness of the gospel and of its demands upon us.

First, the Christian of today has to see the Christian life as a sharing in the life of God in the sense that it is a sharing in the eternal movement of his love which both embraces the world and redeems it. The world and we who inhabit it are the objects of the love of God at all times, but we must not understand that to be so simply in terms of God's beholding us and directing feelings of love and affection towards us. It is very easy for us to think in those terms: we live in a sentimental age and sentimentality consists in enjoying pleasant thoughts about someone or something because it meets a need in us, but without any readiness on our part to accept any obligation towards the object of our sentimentality. The Word of God is 'alive and active'—the Word—the expression of the love of God in the world. He is alive and active to sustain us in being and to bring us to fullness of life through fellowship with himself. We must, therefore, pursue the practice of the habitual awareness of God's activity. The traditional phrase is 'habitual recollection', but perhaps a better word to use is 'awareness'. We use the word 'recollect' to describe the practice of bringing back something from the past which has not only been forgotten but in some sense has become ineffective and is to be recalled to significance. 'Awareness' on the other hand has the sense of becoming conscious of that which is there all the time but which we have been too blind or deaf to see or hear. As we develop this 'habitual awareness' we learn to look at the world and at other people as dependent upon, sustained by and loved by God, even when (in the case of people) they are unconscious of his activity or are living in a way which is clearly contrary to his will. The very fact that they are free to do so is a sign of his love which gives man his freedom. As this awareness becomes part of us, so we find that it is not so much we who are seeking to become aware of the activity of God as that the world and people by their very life and contingency speak to us of him. Pious writers sometimes tell us that we must see God in every little flower crannied in the wall. Some find that difficult to do, and in a sentimental world it can easily confirm a sentimental understanding of God. Theologically it can be justified, in that there is no point in the universe at which God is not, but it is much sounder and just as accurate theologically to think of the flower as speaking to us of the energies of God by which it is created and held in being. To become aware of things or people in this way is not to deny the reality which they possess by being themselves. Rather it is an awareness of the authenticity of their existence which can speak to us of the reality of the love from which it springs and to which it bears witness.

The Christian knows God to be a community of love. He also knows him to be a community which extended its life to embrace creation and to restore it to its true relationship to itself. Because of sin this movement of love involved the cross and the Christian knows himself to be a sharer in that love, not merely through union with Christ but through the cross of Christ. It is for this reason that in his awareness he can face the dark side of creation and does not have to shield his eyes from it or try to evade it. It can speak to him of the redemptive work of God in his love, but it will only do so if his awareness of God is an awareness of him as the Blessed Trinity.

It is for this reason that a Christian must know that worship is Trinitarian and must be helped to experience it as such. It is Trinitarian in two senses. As he comes to worship he is enabled by the power of the Spirit to share in the perfect expression of man's relationship to God as Father wrought out in the life of the incarnate Son, the Word made flesh. But that is only possible through the cross which is itself an act of the Blessed Trinity. So it is that the Christian who has, because of the cross, been united to God in Christ finds himself also called to share in the utterly self-giving love which gave birth to the cross. Of all this the Christian is reminded by his baptism.

> You have been taught that when we were baptized in Christ Jesus we were baptized in his death; in other words, when we were baptized we went into the tomb with him and joined him in death, so that as Christ was raised from the dead by the Father's glory, we too might live a new life.[11]

The Christian life can be summed up as living out the meaning of our baptism by participating in the Eucharist.

This extends to our personal prayer. When we pray we are consciously opening ourselves to allow the prayer of Christ to be prayed in us. This demands sharing his death and resurrection. The way of exchange must be an integral part of our prayer, though at times, of course, this will demand a sharing in Gethsemane as we wrestle to prevent evil from finding a response within us.

With regard to times and seasons for personal prayer, two points must be made. First, we must have periods of silence when we can wait upon God. Silence does not simply mean being quiet and refraining from speech. Nor does it mean that everyone should practise some form of contemplation without words. By silence is meant the conscious effort to shut out the noise of the world in order to become aware of the presence of God and attend to him for his sake allowing the prayer of Christ to be prayed in us. (I think that most of us priests seriously underestimate the difficulties which the ordinary person has to face in finding space and quiet for this and we should be concerned to give much more help in dealing with the problem than we do.) Secondly, the normal way of praying for Christians today should be the frequent use of short and simple prayers so that we learn to acquire an attitude of prayer. It is the kind of praying that is advocated by St Benedict and the author of the *Imitation of Christ*. It need not be consciously Trinitarian, though it will be so in fact, and may take the form of an honest colloquy with the Lord about the difficulties of praying his prayer, such as is practised by Don Camillo in the delightful books by Giovanni Guareschi.[12]

Secondly, the Christian today needs to recover a sense of reverence and awe. The New Testament speaks of the gospel as 'the mystery'. The word is used, not in the popular sense, but to describe that which has been hidden and is now revealed and which is to be known by listening, looking, awareness and obedience. Something of what the word signifies can be understood by thinking of our appreciation of a picture painted by one of the great masters. A knowledge of his life, his background, his technique, the pigments he used, the circumstances in which he came to paint it can all help us to appreciate it, but a true understanding of it will only come if we are prepared to look, wait and receive, allowing it to speak to us. It might seem that, in the case of the mystery of God revealed in Christ, there is a dimension which is not present in the secular sphere, namely that of obedience. But it is to be found even there. We shall not understand the picture if we approach it with preconceived ideas and reject it if it does not conform to them. We must hold ourselves before it with openness of mind and spirit in an alert and disciplined body, if it is to speak to us. Only when we have done so are we so seized by it that we can understand and assess it.

So the Christian mystery has to be understood. It cannot be understood in terms of its usefulness to us nor can it be manipulated to serve our ends. If our critical faculties are exercised in that spirit, what we shall be assessing will be something of our own invention, not the mystery revealed by God. God has revealed his loving design to save all men in Christ, not merely the ancient people of God, the Jews, through their being conformed to the image of his Son.

For this reason, we must not work out our pastoral theology in purely cerebral terms. We must work out ways in which it can be experienced. To this end we must learn to use art and music and appreciate the influence of the physical. The recovery of the use of the rosary in recent years in unexpected quarters and the recognition of the part played by the body in prayer are indications of the need for an approach which is not purely intellectual.[13] To give another personal example, recently, on a pastoral visit to a parish, I was calling upon a simple Cornishwoman in her cottage. I was surprised to see a copy of Salvador Dali's 'Christ of St John of the Cross' hanging on the wall. When I spoke to her about it, she said she often just sat and looked at it and it helped her to pray for the world which was in such a mess. It became evident in conversation that it had also given her a deep understanding of the vocation of the Christian to share in the redeeming love of God.

Thirdly, the Christian today must recover a sense of discipline and sacrifice. The two are closely related but distinct. By a sense of discipline, I mean recognizing that the acquisition of any worth-while skill or wisdom demands hard work and application from which there is no escape. Only in this way is the point reached at which the skill becomes part of the person who is then set free to use that skill creatively. Initially there is a certain pleasure in doing what comes naturally. But after a while we find that we are limited and lack the freedom to develop. It is at this point that we have to learn and practise. The learning, when we put ourselves under an expert, may well involve handling a tool or learning a fingering which at first seems unnatural. It is only later that we discover that it is the right way and that what comes spontaneously does not work beyond a certain point. Many Christians have never got beyond the first stage. Some do not even realize that there is any other and when they find that it does not satisfy simply give up. Others take it seriously for a while but, when the demands become too great, abandon the effort, often because they lack vision.

The secular atmosphere in which we live means that we need more guidelines, more encouragement, more of a framework not less. It is a mark of the man-centredness of secularism to suggest that we are advanced and strong enough to dispense with them. Christians today, priests and laity alike, need a workable and simple pattern of life. They also need clear and specific instruction, not only in the Faith but also on *how* to worship, *how* to receive the Sacraments, *how* to pray, and *how* to use the Scriptures in such a way that they will persevere and grow in the likeness of Christ. Such guidance must be given in such a way as to provide the raw material for loving God and our neighbour and lead those who use it to see the effort they make as a response to the grace of God. In other words the balance must be maintained between Give and Take.

The provision of such a framework and such guidance recognizes that the way of achieving holiness follows the same pattern which must be followed if a human being is to achieve excellence in any other worth-while activity. There are significant differences, the chief of which is that growing in Christian discipleship involves that death to life which we call sacrifice. In a secular age, we have special responsibility to remind Christians that sacrifice is integral to the Christian life. It is irresponsible, faithless and cruel to allow them to think otherwise. At the same time it is not for us to perform the immolation nor to provide occasions for it. What we pastors must do is to prepare Christians for it and equip them with the vision to enable them to embrace the way of the cross.[14]

At the same time, and this is the fourth point about the way of Christian living today, we have to present our pastoral theology in such a manner as to show that we really believe that grace is effective—that God acts and that, by

76

grace, his will can be obeyed. It is particularly necessary to do this with regard to the sacraments. No doubt there was a time when they were abused by a misunderstanding of the scriptural, Catholic and Anglican doctrine of *ex opere operato*[15] by virtue of the work done—and thought of in a mechanical way as if they were effective independently of the response of the recipient. The danger today is that by an unbalanced emphasis upon the way in which the sacraments are performed or the rite and language which are used, the impression is given that their value depends upon the effect upon the worshippers and the extent to which they evoke a response. Too often the sacraments are seen simply as cultic rites designed to edify us and capable of being modified or dispensed with if they do not. It is forgotten that the sacraments are primarily acts of Christ dependent upon his promises, love and power. As the Catechism says, sacraments 'are a means whereby we receive' and 'a pledge to assure us thereof'.

> If we base our assurance of belonging to God only upon passing through certain religious feelings, then our sense of assurance shifts with our shifting feelings. But God's grace is wider and surer than man's emotions. Through a right use of the Sacraments, as pledges of God's love, our certainty is made to depend upon definite outward facts about which there can be no doubt.[16]

They are, as the Articles remind us, effectual signs and, mercifully, not dependent upon the worthiness of the minister. They are, as it were, one side of the coin of which the other is justification by faith. The Eucharist of the New Covenant is given to those who know that they are accepted in the Beloved but find it hard to realize under the pressures of today that they may come, not presuming in their own righteousness but in the manifold and great mercies of God. The tragedy is that with the very proper recovery of the centrality of eucharistic worship throughout the Church, the understanding of it in the mind of the ordinary congregation has become increasingly humanistic. Emphasis is rightly placed today upon the significance of the sacraments in expressing truth about man, such as his relationship to creation and the fact that he is a social being, but the more this is done, the more necessary it becomes to make it evident that the purpose of the Christian life and of the sacraments within it is the consecration of human life by its being taken into God in Christ and that this is primarily the work of God to which man responds.

Generally speaking, we need to tell Christians today to pray above all for grace to enable them to grow in holiness, rather than to tell God about the problems which they think are important and ask him to provide the solution which they think is the right one.

Finally, in the earth-bound society of today we need to give a vision of the eternal purpose for which man is created. The epilogue to the Bible, the Book of Revelation, gives us in the most dramatic and, at times, strange language a pattern of images to reveal the fulfilment of the mystery. We are given a vision of the ultimate purpose for which creation exists. It is the gathering together of all things in one, even in Christ to the praise and glory of God. We see the whole of creation set in a new relationship to God in Christ by the Spirit. Every part, freed from the bondage of corruption, perfectly fulfils itself and does so to the praise of the glory of the grace of God. Man as the vice-regent of creation takes his place in expressing the praises of creation as it reflects back to God his love and holiness.

In this age, creation is opaque. There are dark places, and the glory of God is obscured by the self-centredness of man and his misuse of creation. Creation as a whole does not reflect back to God his beauty, order, majesty and love, for it is marred by the influence of evil. But in Christ man can be redeemed and can then learn to take his part in making creation the sphere of communion with God. The fellowship which we are given with God in Christ here and now is to be lived out in obedience and suffering, but it is not limited to this world. It is to be fulfilled in the world to come at the 'end of the age'. Time will be no more, for we shall be caught up in the ceaseless and eternal life of God, which is both perfect activity and perfect rest.

Of this we can only speak now while stammering for words. Yet we are given glimpses of what shall be. Here and now there are moments when time stands still. The craftsman working with his hands; the lover with his beloved; the ordinary man called to perform an act of heroic compassion; such know what it is to forget the time and to be so absorbed in what they are doing as to forget themselves. Yet afterwards they will say 'This was a moment when I was truly myself.'

In Christ we are to be occupied in the perfect exercise of the whole of our being to the glory of God. We shall forget ourselves in him, yet we shall be truly ourselves, expressing with all the saints what is the breadth and length and height and depth of the love of Christ which surpasses knowledge, that we may be filled with all the fullness of God.

Habitual awareness of God alive and active, the sense of mystery, discipline and sacrifice, a realization of the power of grace and a vision of our eternal destiny: these, I believe, are the qualities which are needed for an authentic way of Christian living today. Clearly they have to be clothed with flesh and blood, to be given concrete shape. While, here and there, ways in which this may be done have been hinted at, to do this is essentially the task of the local pastor with his own flock whom he should know by name and for whom he should be prepared, if need be, to spend his life. It is to him that this book has been dedicated with the prayer that it may help him in his vocation.

NOTES

Chapter 1

1. Rom. 1: 1–2.
2. Gal. 1: 7.
3. Rom. 15: 15–16.
4. Rom. 16: 25–7.
5. 1 Cor. 6: 15.
6. 1 Cor. 10: 14–22.
7. The importance of non-theological factors in the life of the Church is brought out strongly in Paul Johnson, *A History of Christianity*, Penguin 1978. Although at times such factors seem to be stressed at the expense of the spiritual forces directing and influencing the Church, the book provides a valuable balance to the predominantly ecclesiastical approach of many church histories.
8. John Ruef, *Paul's First Letter to Corinth* (Penguin 1971), p. xix.
9. 2 Cor. 4: 10.
10. Hubert Richards, *St Paul and his Epistles. A New Introduction* (Darton, Longman and Todd 1979), p. 70.
11. Patrick Masterson, *Atheism and Alienation* (Penguin 1973), p. 14.
12. Op. cit., p. 72.
13. 1 Cor. 9: 21.
14. Martin Thornton, *My God* (Hodder and Stoughton 1974), p. 16.
15. There is an urgent need for a critical examination of Christian experience in the light of recent work on religious experience and human consciousness, particularly in the light of post-

Einsteinian understanding of reality. See for example, Alastair Hardy, *The Spiritual Nature of Man*, OUP 1979. Harold K. Schilling, *The New Consciousness in Science and Religion*, SCM 1973. Lawrence LeShan, *Clairvoyant Reality*, Turnstone Press, 1980 (previously published in 1974 as *The Medium, The Mystic and the Scientist*). F.C. Happold, *Religious Faith and Twentieth-Century Man*, new edn, Darton, Longman and Todd 1980. Much writing on religious experience today reflects a dualist approach which contrasts the spiritual and material rather than a sacramental understanding of the way in which man in the whole of his being and the universe are consecrated in the incarnate Christ.

16. R. H. Fuller, *The Foundations of New Testament Christology* (Fontana 1969), p. 248.
17. Philip Sherrard, *Christianity and Eros* (SPCK 1976), p. 49.
18. Dietrich Bonhoeffer, *The Cost of Discipleship* (SCM, rev. edn), p. 206 (italics in original).
19. N. Clark, *An Approach to the Theology of the Sacraments* (SCM 1956), pp. 83–4.
20. This prayer is printed as the quotation at the beginning of Chapter 2 in M. C. D'Arcy, *The Mind and Heart of Love*, Faber 1945. I am encouraged by the fact that Fr Kenneth Leech in his admirable book *True Prayer*, Sheldon Press 1980, has also used it as an example of the way in which prayer can become a way of 'reinforcing one's own status, needs and values'.
21. 'Choruses from "The Rock" VI. *Collected Poems 1909–1962* (Faber 1974), p. 174.
22. Articles of Religion. Article IX.
23. *The Celebration of Flesh* (Peter Smith 1965), p. 87.

Chapter 2
1. *An Humbler Heaven* (Fount 1977), p. 29.
2. It is interesting to contrast the use which is made by some Christian moralists today of the 'naturalization fallacy', which denies the possibility of passing from 'is' to 'ought', with the readiness with which those who wish to discredit religion or morality use the discovery of an ancient document or a new

scientific technique to justify sweeping assertions about the validity of religious or ethical beliefs. The Christian belief that the God who revealed Himself in Christ is the God who created the universe, including man as a psychosomatic unity, means that there is a relation between 'is' and 'ought' but that it consists neither in a dualism which divorces the spiritual and moral from the material, nor in a determinism based on an assumption that the material constitutes the whole of reality.

3. *The Secularization of the European Mind in the Nineteenth Century* (CUP 1975), p. 38.
4. *Suffering* (Darton, Longman and Todd 1973), p. 131.
5. *The Mastery of Evil* (Bles, 3rd rev. ed. 1944), pp. 28–9.
6. Gal 5: 19–23.
7. *Certain Difficulties felt by Anglicans in Catholic Teaching*, II. (Longmans, Green & Co.), p. 250.
8. John Colville, *Footprints in Time* (Collins 1976), p. 277.
9. Op. cit., p. 62.
10. Op. cit., p. ix.
11. 'Choruses from the Rock VI', *Collected Poems 1909–1962* (Faber 1974), p. 174.
12. 1 Cor. 12: 12–21.
13. Canon E. L. Mascall has made this point with his customary lucidity and cogency in his latest book where he discusses the difference of sexuality:
'Differentation is [thus] inherent in the unity of mankind, not inconsistent with it. But this does not mean that the various human differentiations—familial, racial, cultural, national and the rest—do not need unceasing vigilance if they are to be kept in their right relations with one another or that anyone of them may not be destructive of the unity if it becomes hypertrophied, distorted or parasitic.' *Whatever Happened to the Human Mind?* (SPCK 1980), p. 130.
14. The mathematician and theoretical physicist, Professor Freeman Dyson, suggests that perhaps the central problem in humanity's future is how we are to make our social institutions flexible enough to preserve our precious biological and cultural diversity. See his remarkable autobiography *Disturbing the Uni-*

verse (Harper and Row 1979), especially Chapter 20, 'Clades and Clones'.
15. *Dictionary of Christian Ethics* (SCM 1967), s.v. 'Envy', p. 107.
16. *The Complete Poems of Emily Dickinson* (Faber 1973), no. 501.
17. Dorothee Soelle, op. cit., p. 38
18. *The Wound of Knowledge* (Darton, Longman and Todd 1979), pp. 11–12.

Chapter 3
1. Ps. 139: 6–7 (Coverdale version).
2. Ps. 88: 5–6.(Coverdale version).
3. Hosea 11: 1, 4.
4. Eph., 1: 3–7.
5. *Encyclopaedia of Theology* (Burns and Oates 1975), s.v. 'Trinity Divine', p. 1755.
6. Mark 1: 11.
7. *On the Baptism of Christ*, Homily 39.
8. *Jerome Bible Commentary* (Geoffrey Chapman 1968), s.v. 'The Gospel according to Mark'. Edward J. Malley, S. J. 42. 10.
9. Op. cit., 42, 55.
10. John 15: 15.
11. John 16: 13–15.
12. John 17: 21.
13. John 17: 26.
14. Gal. 3: 26–7.
15. Gal. 4: 5–7.
16. 2 Cor. 4: 4. Cf. Col. 1: 15.
17. 2 Cor. 12: 4.
18. Rom. 6: 3, 4, 12.
19. 1 John 1: 3.
20. 1 John 1: 6.
21. 1 John 4: 16.
22. *Theological Investigations*, vol. iv (Darton, Longman and Todd 1966), 'Remarks on the Dogmatic Treatise "De Trinitate" ', p. 79.
23. *Invaded by God—Mysticism and the Indwelling Trinity* (Dimension Books 1979), p. 6.

24. *Agape and Eros*. English translation, rev. edn, 1953.
25. *Passion and Society*. Faber, English translation rev. edn, 1956.
26. *The Mind and Heart of Love*. Faber 1945.
27. Op. cit., p. 40.
28. Op. cit., p. 14.
29. Op. cit., p. 15.
30. Op. cit., p. 16.
31. John 17: 23.
32. 2 Cor. 5: 19.
33. As I have written elsewhere: 'Much modern debate about Christology ignores the moral implications of our understanding of the person of Christ. When I reflect on the incarnation then as a finite human being I expect my mind to be stretched and accept that the mystery will transcend my comprehension. But I do not expect to have my moral sense offended. And, as I have written elsewhere, any statement about the person of Christ which does not seek to express that he is both truly God as well as truly man, leaves me with a religion which offends my moral sense as a human being. I could admire and reverence the wonderful life of the man, Jesus, though as less than God. I could not give him the unconditional adoration which I can give to God alone. But more than that: Jesus would be before me on the cross as the victim of an unyielding God who demanded that such a man should live and die. Easter would no longer be the glorious demonstration of the ultimate victory of love. It would become a demonstration by man that he could conquer in spite of the way in which God had made him and the world. I would indeed find it incredible that such a God should have my loving adoration as the end of my being.' 'Is Christianity Credible? (6)' (*Epworth Review*, vol. vi, no. 2, May 1979).
34. *The Orthodox Way* (Mowbray 1979), p. 27.

Chapter 4
1. *Suffering* (Darton, Longman and Todd 1973), pp. 36–8.
2. Op. cit., p. 119.
3. Heb. 12: 2.

4. 1 Pet. 2: 21–4.
5. *The Gospel is for Everyone*. Church Union, rev. edn, 1976.
6. SPCK 1975.
7. *The Wound of Knowledge*. Darton, Longman and Todd 1979.
8. Op. cit., p. 21.
9. Op. cit., p. 94.
10. Op. cit., p. 117.
11. Rom. 6: 2–4.
12. In my experience the honesty, realism and spontaneity of Don Camillo's conversations with the Lord make these books very useful in teaching Confirmation candidates to pray.
13. On the Jesus Prayer rosary, two books may be especially recommended: Kallistos Ware, *The Power of the Name* (Fairacres Publications) and Per-Olof Sjögren, *The Jesus Prayer* (SPCK). On the traditional Western rosary *Five for Sorrow Ten for Joy* by the Methodist, Neville Ward (SPCK), is very good. Excellent advice on the disciplined use of the body is given in a little book by H. Caffarel, *The Body at Prayer* (SPCK).
14. Sacrifice is not only integral to the Christian life. It is integral to human life. Too often it is understood simply as obedience to God as lawgiver. Scripture takes us forward from such an understanding to one in which it is seen as springing from the nature of God as love. It is in this light that we must understand the sacrifice of the cross itself and the sacrifice which Christians are called to offer and which they are enabled to offer through the cross. The latter must be seen as the expression of that sharing in the love of God, through which the human instinct to love is redeemed and fulfilled.
15. Article XXV of the Thirty-nine Articles in its original form in the forty-two Articles included a phrase condemning the doctrine of grace *ex opere operato*. The phrase was removed in the revision of 1563.

(i) Originally the phrase conveyed a true and valuable idea. *Opus operatum* was contrasted with *opus operantis* and implies that the efficacy of all sacraments depends upon the appointment of their author, God, and not on the merit of the officiant or recipient . . . It vindicates the important truth that grace is God's free gift. We do not earn or create it by our own faith or moral efforts.

(ii) This became corrupted into the idea condemned in this Article that sacraments conferred grace automatically, quite apart from the faith or penitence of the recipient. In this sense, it was rightly condemned in the first edition of this Article . . . the blessing that he personally receives must depend upon our individual capacity for receiving it, namely, our true repentance, our real belief in Christ and his promises, our desire to surrender ourselves to him, and to employ the grace that He bestows. It has been said 'The grace of Sacraments does not depend on our faith but for its effect in us all depends upon our faith'; and again 'Grace without faith may come upon us but it cannot make us holy.' This second truth was secured by the language of the Article and the condemnation of the phrase (*s.c. ex opere operato*) was wisely withdrawn since it contained a true meaning as well as a false. E. J. Bicknell, *A Theological Introduction to the Thirty Nine Articles of the Church of England,*. rev. H. J. Carpenter (Longmans, Green & Co., 1955), p. 386. The balance expressed in this Article and Article XXVI needs to be recovered at the present time.

16. Op. cit., p. 358.

INDEX OF SCRIPTURAL
REFERENCES

INDEX OF PROPER NAMES